BRINGING DEATH TO LIFE

An Uplifting Exploration of Living, Dying, the Soul Journey and the Afterlife

Patricia Scanlan • Dr. Mary Helen Hensley
Aidan Storey • Pamela Young

Cover and interior design by Frame25 Productions
Cover photo © Ase c/o Shutterstock.com

Published by:
Rainbow Ridge Books, LLC
1056 Commodore Drive
Virginia Beach, VA 23454
www.rainbowridgebooks.com

If you are unable to order this book from your local bookseller, you may order directly from the distributor.

Square One Publishers, Inc.
115 Herricks Road
Garden City Park, NY 11040
(877) 900-BOOK

Library of Congress Control Number: 2019942797

ISBN 978-1-937907-63-1

10 9 8 7 6 5 4 3 2 1

Printed in India through Nutech Print Services

To the mothers, the fathers, and all who have gone before us, who guide and inspire us.

Dear Reader,

Thank you so much for taking this journey with us. Our aim is to encourage an "intimacy" with death or, as the poet and writer John O'Donohue calls it, the "Unknown Companion" with whom we all travel from the moment of our birth.

Before we introduce ourselves, and start on our exploration of the book's theme, we would like to emphasise that our beliefs are just that: beliefs. We don't expect everyone to share them, or to agree on every aspect.

Our only wish is that in the pages of this book, as we broach the theme of death with openness and love, something will resonate with you, easing any fears you might have and hopefully bringing you comfort. If that is the case, then our job is done.

With love and blessings,

Patricia, Aidan, Pamela and Mary Helen

Contents

"Once the soul awakens,
the search begins and
you can never go back."

—from *Anam Cara* by John O' Donohue

Introduction

Death, A Life Companion

Patricia

I first became "intimate" with Death when my beloved mother passed in 2007. Until then, like most people, I'd lost relatives, much-loved aunts, uncles, cousins, neighbours. I'd attended funerals, cried when the coffins were carried out of the church and laid in the cold, loamy soil of the grave. Then I'd gone home and carried on with my life, feeling sadness for the loss but not dwelling too much on it as life carried on at its usual fast pace.

Before I talk about the effect of my parents' deaths on my life, I'll give a bit of background on how I came to be interested in the theme of death, and connected with my wonderful friends and co-authors of this book.

I'll start at the beginning. My first novel, *City Girl*, was published in 1990 and in the years that followed I achieved professional success, selling millions of books and being taken far out of my comfort zone. I did many media interviews and wrote dozens of articles. I made speeches at publishing conferences, in exotic locations, as a guest of my publishers, travelled on book tours, conducted hundreds of signing sessions, and continued to write my novels despite the numerous demands that were made on my time.

Like all of us, I was presented with challenges in life, and sometimes struggled to make sense of it. But at that time, I would not have described myself as Spiritually awakened.

My first realisation that there was another dimension to my life came when I attended the renowned acupuncturist Dr Annette Tallon, who had trained in Singapore and whose reputation for sterling work was unparalleled in Ireland. Under her gentle tutelage, I began to remember the ancient truths I'd long forgotten in this life. She gave me a copy of *The Game of Life and How to Play It*, by Florence Scovel Shinn. Reading it changed my life.

It was during a big book-trade event, held by my publishers, that I was introduced to someone else who changed my ways of thinking. I still remember poet, philosopher and writer John O'Donohue shaking my hand and smiling at me: I felt I knew him.

We started chatting and it was as though everyone else wafted away, so engrossed were we in our conversation."

I read his internationally bestselling book *Anam Cara*, Gaelic for "soul friend," and discovered that when old soul friends meet each other there is an instant recognition. Then I understood why I felt I'd always known him. Between us, there was that instant "reconnection and recognition."

At that time in my life, I was enveloped in misery at the ending of a relationship with a man I'd thought was "the one." Yet, while the chapters on solitude in that book gave comfort, it was the passages on death that most resonated with me.

"There is a presence who walks the road of life with you," he writes. "When you were born it came out of the womb with you: with the excitement of your arrival, nobody noticed." The name of your companion is, of course, Death.

In his chapter on "The Unknown Companion," the author's opening line is stunning in its revelation: "There is a presence who walks the road of life with you," he writes. "When you were born it came out of the womb with you: with the excitement of your arrival, nobody noticed."

The name of your companion is, of course, Death.

John O'Donohue wrote powerfully about fear, and dealing with it, and about the negativity that surrounds death, as we know it: "Though death is the most powerful and ultimate experience in one's life, our culture goes to great pains to deny its presence."

The cult of "immortality" is preferable to facing reality.

A bookseller I spoke to about *Bringing Death to Life* said how pleased she was that "Death" was in the title. She said it drove her mad when people said they had "lost" someone. "Where? On the street? In the supermarket? Death is death," she said, "no matter what euphemisms are used to describe it."

My own first intimate experience with death—the moment when "Before" became "After"—was my mother's passing.

Although it was ten years since I'd read *Anam Cara*, the profound and innate Celtic Spiritual wisdom of John O'Donohue's writings flooded back and I remembered at a deep, cellular level how to assist my mother with her passing. It wasn't about my grief, or my longing to prevent her from going, it was about her journey, being with her, supporting and encouraging her as she crossed the threshold that we will all cross eventually.

John O'Donohue's great gift to me, as well as his friendship, was to enable me to become intimate with the death process. To partake in it, which is empowering. When you give your loved one permission to go, you are not a helpless voyeur: you are an active participant at this life-changing event, and the comfort this brings in the desolate days afterwards cannot be underestimated.

My precious mother helped me lose my fear of death and, almost ten years later, when I was privileged to assist my dad on his homeward journey, I wanted to share this knowledge: that the more intimate we become with death, the lifetime companion, the less intimidating and fearful it becomes. Death is not the end: it's just a change from what we know. Relationships with our departed loved ones continue if we want them to. We are not powerless: we can include them in every aspect of our lives, and they are only a thought away.

I could think of no better collaborators to write this book with than the *anam cairde* I'm honoured to have in this lifetime: Aidan Storey, Pamela Young and Dr Mary Helen

Hensley. We have shared many lifetimes together. They have profound knowledge and experience of death, and life beyond the veil. When you have read this book, dear reader, I know that, while you will still grieve a loss or worry about your own mortality, death might lose its fear for you. The beginnings of intimacy with this life companion will set you on a journey that will bring death to life, for you, in ways you could never have imagined.

Aidan

I was born in 1958, raised in the suburbs of Dublin, and now live in Kildare. I was the youngest of seven, a much-loved, happy child, who enjoyed family life and all the usual rough-and-tumble games I played with family and friends in my garden. The only difference was that when my friends left and the garden was quiet, angels visited me. I continue to have a wonderful connection with them. My autobiography, *Angels of Divine Light*, goes into great detail about my angelic experiences. My angels guide me in my work, my writings, and in every aspect of my life.

I was never afraid of these beautiful Spirits as I was told from a very young age that my angels would always look after me, especially when I was alone. It wasn't until much later that I realised not everyone could see what I could. Little did I know then that my happy, carefree life would turn into one of misery and torment. The angels helped me to claw my way back from the pain and abuse, that dark place of the soul, into which I was plunged.

Through their powerful love and healing, I overcame hardship and sorrow, and was able to use my experiences of abuse to help many others who had suffered in their own lives.

Over the years I have learned to communicate with my angels. They have taught me many things and shown me how to look at life and death in a much simpler way. In the same way they give me guidance for my clients to help and direct them on the soul's journey and bring love and healing into their lives. In this book, I hope I can bring this message to you in the same simple form.

Death was not something my family or friends discussed very often. It was a taboo subject. To talk about death was considered to tempt Fate and who would want to do that?

Yet we were brought up with death. It was a natural part of life. My mother, who looked after many of the elderly in the area, often sat with them while they were dying. When they had passed, she would wash and lay them out. She never had any fear of dying or the process of death.

She would come home, tell us who had died and that they had had "a lovely death." "I held their hand as they passed over and it was so peaceful and gentle," she would say. That was the extent of what I knew about death. She also told us that if you were bad you'd go to Hell when you died.

My aunty Bibby, who was great fun, would sometimes joke when she called in to tell us a neighbour or friend had died. When we asked what they had died from, she would look at us and say, "A shortness of breath," then laugh and repeat it. "A shortness of breath. That's what everybody dies of!"

Patricia—or Tricia as we call her—once told me that when she asked her father what an acquaintance had died of, he looked her straight in the eye and said, "He died of a Tuesday," and burst out laughing. That generation took death in their stride.

The angels tell me that death is nothing to fear, not the end but a continuation of the soul journey and the path of learning.

Perhaps because of that I never feared death, and often when I was younger, utterly depressed and miserable, I prayed for God to take me. But now I know that wasn't part of the Divine plan for my soul journey. When my time is up, God will call me. Then my Spirit and soul will hear and go freely. The angels tell me that death is nothing to fear, not the end but a continuation of the soul journey and the path of learning. During each lifetime the soul learns and experiences more, rising to a new level of awareness and understanding. When the time is right it will be reborn, either into the same soul family or a new one, with different lessons to learn.

In this book, I write about my experiences with the loss of my parents and the grief I felt or, in the case of my dad, did not feel. I tell of my first experience of death, and witnessing the death of a child, and what the angels told me about life after death. I tell about the Spirit visit I had from a young man, who had committed suicide, during a session with his mother—she had come to me for help. I talk about practical things, too, like the importance of making a will, and how to move on from the grieving process. I hope my experiences will bring you some comfort and help, that this book will ease the pain of loss, if you are experiencing it, and take away the fear of death, which can cause unnecessary distress.

Pamela

I was born in 1948 to my mother, Evelyn, whose entire life was dedicated to Spirit. As a child she saw and played happily with the Spirits of deceased children, and later, as a young woman, she developed the gift of channelling messages from Spirit.

My childhood was filled with the presence and love of the spirit world. I was brought up with a simple philosophy devoid of dogma, just the knowledge that God is love, that we are never alone, that we are constantly guided by Spirit, and live on after death. I was taught that we were born to fulfil "The Work"—a concept channelled through my mother regarding humanity's spiritual path, which was on the brink of great change in bringing Heaven to Earth. We were asked to be careful of our thoughts as thought is a living thing, and "It will come true." I had complete faith in "The Work" and was truly blessed to have my mam and the love of Spirit to guide and nurture me.

Even as a youngster, I had knowledge and indirect experience of where we go after death, informed by my mother's work as a Spiritual medium. She channelled many things about the spirit world, the wonderful opportunities people have to heal and grow, the exquisite beauty of the place and what happens after death. I was aware that I had Spirit friends helping and guiding me.

Mam had written about her Spiritual gift, and her childhood memories of communicating with so-called dead people. After her death, I found the piece in an exercise book.

She talked of her awakening as a ten-year-old to the life of Spirits, including playing with Spirit children in a cellar in her childhood home. Later I will say more about my mother's gifts and insights, which included astral travelling.

My own life had its challenges and my own understanding of death came out of these times, specifically following a near-death experience.

Four decades ago, I was divorced and a single mum to my young son and daughter. It was a huge struggle financially. I lived miles away from my family, and although I was blessed with my lovely children and had a job that allowed me freedom for the school holidays, times were hard.

One weekend, my kids were away at their dad's when I fell into a sudden deep depression, overwhelmed with the anxiety of trying to keep everything going. My best friend was away with her family, as was my mother, and back then there were no mobile phones.

I would never consider suicide but I wanted to be free of stress and loneliness. And that weekend I was completely alone and lonely. That night I prayed for help. I went to bed feeling beaten, little knowing that I was about to have an experience that has remained with me to this day, such was its beauty, radiance and clarity. It was all the more remarkable for the fact that it rose out of the ashes of utter dejection.

It confirmed what I had been told as a child, that death is not the end. What had been a "faith" became a "knowing." As I lay in bed, swamped in loss, desolation and failure, I had the sensation that I was slowly receding into my body, as if I was sinking. As I sank, I felt as if I was going down through my body, then through the bed and the floor. I was not asleep but neither was I aware of being in my bed. I was conscious only of travelling downwards, in utter despair, for a long time, then becoming aware not only of my own but also other people's pain. It was a dark place. I felt unwell as I drew closer to the needs of others. It was as if they wanted my attention and my attachment, and it was difficult to pull myself away.

Just as I thought I could no longer tolerate the intense nausea, I started to feel a subtle change. I seemed to be rising on a slight incline, and as I did so, my anguish, and that of others, fell away. Eventually I levelled out and was floating vertically, aware of a pinprick of light in the far distance. Gradually I progressed towards it—it was like a magnet drawing me closer.

I began to shed the feelings of loss, worry and anxiety as an extraordinary peace enfolded me. I had never before experienced such total serenity. I felt a tremendous healing take place. The rays of light were bathing me, pulling me further into their ever-increasing circle, creating a sense of exhilaration. I was going home.

The light enveloped me. In fact, it was far more than that. I wasn't separated from the light. It was *me.*

For the first time ever, I did not need anyone else to make me feel loved, or alive, or to give me an identity or reason for living. I was *love.* It was a self-replenishing love, devoid of the need to give or receive, to give me purpose, or make me feel worthy in the act of loving another. On the contrary, I felt self*less.* I was at one and connected to everything and everyone in love. I was pure, unconditional love and I was *home*!

I felt a tremendous healing take place. The rays of light were bathing me, pulling me further into their ever-increasing circle, creating a sense of exhilaration. I was going home.

As I was basking in the bliss, a giant of a man appeared before me in shining white robes. I experienced an even higher sense of love and peace. I was at one with this soul, with whom I knew I shared an extraordinary level of awareness. Although he did not speak, I felt his great compassion and love for me as he pointed his finger, indicating I should return to my life. It was not my time.

It had taken an age to get to that sublime realm but only an instant to arrive back in my bed. I was in a cold sweat and felt I was almost dead, the polar opposite to what I had felt in Heaven. I cried until I fell into a deep, healing sleep.

Waking and remembering was a wonder and a longing. I prayed with the deepest gratitude for the gift of that communion.

As Carl Jung once said, "No longer did I believe in God—I knew him." I also knew I could heal as I had been healed.

That experience changed the direction of my life. Within three years, I was living in Horwich in the north of England, with my children, having secured a place on a degree course that would lead to my career in social work.

Now I could start my conscious Earthly journey back to the light. I joined the weekly healing group at my local church, where I trained to channel the healing gift with integrity. I also did Reiki. I now do absent healing, sending prayers for people. Increasingly I felt the presence of a feminine divinity around me. The more I meditated and entered the silence, the greater my connection with her became. I now call her the Lady of Light and I know she walks with and holds every soul in love and light.

Humanity has always been in service to healing and bringing light, but now I know without doubt that our main mission is to heal our self: in so doing we heal the world. We begin by healing our mind of emotional wounds and negative thoughts to uncover our true selves as radiant beings of love and light.

All my life I have had an unflinching faith and trust in "The Work." I now call it "the work of love and light," and, dear reader, I'm happy to share with you my firm belief and knowledge that death is not the end: our souls are ever-evolving.

Mary Helen

As someone who has had extremely heightened senses from birth, my life as a kinaesthetic (touch), auditory (sound) and visual clairvoyant has been anything but ordinary. Nurtured and protected by my parents, I had kept my little secret for at least two decades until destiny would no longer allow the illusion. I had always had prophetic dreams, communicated regularly with those in Spirit, including my long-deceased grandfather "Judge," and often knew things would happen before they took place, but they all came together on the day my life changed forever: 14 December 1991.

The day I died.

A high-speed driver's-side impact crushed my vehicle, and my body, releasing my Spirit from the Earth plane in a single heartbeat. The collision took place after time had virtually ground to a halt, allowing me to decide whether I would go through the experience inside or outside my physical body. I recall having that choice, which speaks volumes.

As the story goes, I left my body seconds before the accident, just in time to witness my death. I saw everything that took place below me: the seat folded in half beneath me and my head smashed the window out. My entire left side was crushed by the driver's door, now in the shape of the front of the car that hit me. People gathered and an ambulance was called, all while I had a bird's eye view of the spectacle.

In this world, the music, the vibrations, the colours, the feeling that comes only with the freedom of releasing the human form leaves me with no adequate way to describe its all-encompassing beauty.

A low drone, a blinding flash of light and suddenly I was somewhere else. In this world, the music, the vibrations, the colours, the feeling that comes only with the freedom of releasing the human form leaves me with no adequate way to describe its all-encompassing beauty.

I reunited with my guides, the beings who had watched me from another realm during the life I had just left, as well as all of the lives before and around it. I was home, or somewhere closer to home than I had ever experienced on Earth. Bathed in colour and light, I examined the twenty-one years I had left behind. Permeated with love, I studied my performance, feeling gratitude for everyone who had played a part in my story.

During what he described as a "celestial" visit before my birth, my father had been promised that mine would be an unusual and lengthy life, so I knew that the accident had been a temporary interlude to change the way I was currently living. My gifts would be enhanced and could no longer be kept quiet. If I chose the path of stewardship, my guides assured me that support of a miraculous nature would become available to me. I was also promised that most of the information shared with me during my "death" would remain in my memory. I would return to life with details of what it means for the body to die and what awaits who we really are. As much as I would have loved to stay in the Divine presence of that love, I knew I was going back.

Armed with the knowledge of many lives and deaths, and the serenity that comes from remembering we are all timeless creators of our own reality, I made the choice to re-engage with my broken body. Every injury I received would serve as a reminder that I had been given the chance to live again in this life as Mary Helen. Eventually I chronicled these events in my book, *Promised by Heaven*, laying my soul bare and sharing my stories with anyone who had "the ears" to hear them. I have dedicated my life to teaching people that death is nothing to fear, that we already are that which we seek: Divine beings who came from perfection to experience what it means to be human: the good, the bad, the beautiful and the ugly.

Somewhere along the way, as we lost touch with our Divinity, we began to fear death. Avoiding it has become a billion-dollar industry. We live in a quick-fix world, with medical treatment available for the illnesses brought on by our lack of attention to wellness, yet we don't educate ourselves about how to make the best of life while we are in good health. Healthcare professionals are run off their feet because *everything* is a crisis now.

I had a middle-aged woman in my office not long ago who explained to me, as I was taking her medical history, that she took more than forty tablets each day. She had no idea what half of them were supposed to be doing for her. How on Earth could she have any quality of life when she spends her days avoiding death? Society has replaced the pursuit of a good-quality life with the absurd belief that quantity outweighs substance.

To live and die well: wouldn't that be a great achievement? What's the first step? Get comfortable talking about death. So many awkward scenes have played out in countless family dynamics because no one wants to discuss it. I have worked with families that were torn apart because of how a loved one was cared for at the end of their life; arguments about how finances and inheritances were ultimately divided and even what music *wasn't* played at a funeral service.

My interest in contributing to this book stems from my desire to show you that if death is no longer treated like an unwelcome and uninvited guest, avoided and hidden until circumstances demand that it is dealt with, you will avoid so much pain and heartache.

It wasn't so very long ago that our ancestors heralded death with the same reverence and delight that we celebrate a birth. They are simply two different points on the same beam of light. Any primary-school kid who has ever taken a basic science class can tell you that matter cannot be created or destroyed. How quickly we forget.

I don't intend to ask you to be happy and excited about dying: with each loss of life comes loss of relationships, some close to the heart and others difficult. The idea is to help swing the pendulum away from extreme avoidance of this inevitable topic and back towards a more balanced acceptance, so that speaking of death and all that accompanies it isn't so uncomfortable. My hope is that in each story at least one nugget of wisdom will shine a little light on death to offer you a fresh outlook on a subject that is an integral part of the circle of life.

Speaking of circles, the four of us—Tricia, Pam, Aidan and I—returned to our soul-friends circle to write this book together. It was, we know, pre-planned before we reincarnated into this world. Aidan is the group's Great Connector. We met through our work and he introduced me to Tricia who, as he anticipated, would become a firm friend. It was she who told me of Pamela, and after I'd read her book, *Hope Street*, I realised why Tricia had been so eager for us to meet. While our background stories were different, the tone of our message was identical. We had the same objective in wanting to help people release their fears and return to love. When we finally met, it was one of those "Nice to see you *again*" moments.

One of the greatest joys in my life is the love of my soul-friends circle. Now we are co-authoring this book in a spirit of love and friendship, and hope that our combined knowledge and experience of death will start a discussion that brings death to its rightful place in life. Hold on to your hats as we lift the veil on death, the final frontier.

Affirmation to Accept Death as a Life Companion

I accept death as my life companion
It exists not to frighten me, but to befriend me
Not to haunt me, but to enlighten me
I recognise that it is not the end, but only a step on an eternal journey of light, from which I have come,
and to which I will return
Nothing is lost, that will not be returned.

"Life takes you to
unexpected places,
love brings you Home."

—Proverb

Preparing to Pass

Patricia

In the taboo surrounding death, too often we do not discuss its stages. If a loved one is gravely ill, we find ways of sidestepping the question that is perhaps to the foremost of our minds—often out of fear, a sense of dread or grief, or an uneasy sense that it is somehow wrong to look at the subject directly: are they dying? If so, how do we know? Do they know they are dying? If so, do they wish to talk about it directly? How long do they have?

As my co-authors show, the person who is dying may or may not be actively engaged with this fact—on a conscious level. However, on a deeper, unconscious, or soul level they absolutely know, and as they prepare to pass, seemingly drifting ever further away from us, their souls are involved in the work of separating from the body, for the next stage of a journey that knows no end.

Learning to "Listen" to the Spirit and the Body

When my dad entered hospital for the last time, I knew he was fading. He had had several near misses, when we were convinced that "this was it", but had always pulled through. We had christened him Lazarus. He had struggled heroically and stoically through dreadful pain and discomfort, especially in the last year of his life. We were in awe of how he maintained his good humour and sense of fun almost to the last. We were blessed that he was *compos mentis*, and made his own decisions concerning his finances, his hospital treatment and other matters until he slipped into unconsciousness two days before he died.

As they prepare to pass, apparently drifting ever further away from us, their souls are involved in the work of separating from the body, for the next stage of a journey that knows no end.

That last stay in hospital, there were many changes in him, and I knew instinctively that he was preparing to let go and join my mother. My dad had always had a healthy appetite. My mother used to say that the only time she worried about him was if he wasn't eating. A rare occurrence and a sign that he really wasn't well.

While his appetite had decreased over the years, Dad still enjoyed a tasty meal, and even when he was in hospital, I always cooked a brunch for us on Saturday or Sunday mornings. One of the things he really relished was streaky bacon, fried crispy.

One such Sunday morning, during his last stay in hospital, I had wrapped his rashers in tinfoil, then headed off to the hospital around nine thirty a.m. He'd have them before the televised Mass he liked to watch. There was no traffic on the road as I whizzed through Fairview, anxious that his treat would still be hot when he got it. It gave me such pleasure to see him enjoy the snack, and I was happy when I went home later in the day that I had done something for him that gave him pleasure, and let him know how special he was to me. (I wasn't so happy a couple of days later when I got a letter through the post telling me I had acquired three points on my licence for speeding. I was about eight m.p.h. over the limit. I never told him.)

The time came, though, when he didn't want to eat, or drink the cup of hot chocolate I brought him every day from the little shop in the hospital foyer. I felt sick at heart as I knew what was happening. All he wanted was soup, and even though we would urge him to have the bread roll with it, he didn't want it. He might take a couple of spoonfuls of jelly for his dessert.

It's very difficult to watch your loved one refusing food and stepping back from all that was once a source of pleasure to them. But the signs had begun long before that.

When Dad decided to cancel the daily delivery of his paper, several months before he went into the hospital for the last time, my stomach lurched. A regular cover-to-cover reader of *The Irish Times*, with his love of crosswords, I knew then that he had started his preparations for setting aside the interests and concerns of this world.

Dad was extremely knowledgeable, and had a great grasp of current affairs, with the added perspective of ninety years of life experience. It included the Second World War, when he had been a very young merchant seaman on a hospital ship during fighting around Salerno and Anzio. Despite their Red Cross markings and being lit up like a Christmas tree, his ship, the *St Andrew*, had been bombed. He'd watched her sister ship, the *St David*, go down during the same raid, and knew that my mother's brother was lost.

His stories of the North Atlantic convoys, where the ships dodged German U-boats, never stopping to pick up survivors if a ship was hit, were heart-rending and gripping. His life at sea was a rich tapestry, and his travels around the globe on the seven seas made me envious as I compared my pale palette of experiences to his vibrant and varied one.

When he told me one day, not long before he died, that he had seen his parents across the room while his leg ulcers were being dressed, I knew the end was not far away.

I had spoken to someone whose care he was under, and asked specifically was my dad dying. Even though at one level I knew he was, I wanted to hear it said out loud by a healthcare professional. No, I was told. His symptoms were a result of the very heavy antibiotics he was on.

"When do you stop the treatment and let nature and Spirit take their course?" I asked.

The medical person wasn't having any of this. They could still pull Dad through. It was all about getting the medication right. For what? I asked. So that he could be in constant pain and discomfort while they tried to balance the heart tablets with the kidney medication? Dad was in the fourth stage of congestive heart failure, and also suffering renal failure. I remembered what a nurse had said to me, almost ten years previously, when I had insisted that my mother's wish for no intervention be followed after a procedure she'd agreed to hadn't worked.

"But she's your *mother*!" the nurse exclaimed, as though I was casually writing Mam off.

"It was *her* wish," I said, "and she was *adamant* about it. We can't ignore her wish." I was angry with that nurse that she would say such a thing to me on a terrible day of grief, shock and exhaustion. I wanted my mother to live, we all did, but not in a way that would have left her infirm for the rest of her days. Even though it broke my heart as they withdrew the antibiotics and other drugs, it was not about us. It was about what was right for her.

Now my dad was making his Earthly preparations to go, and the medical person couldn't admit to it, or perhaps even see it. "He sees his parents in the room with him," I said, feeling I was banging my head off a brick wall.

"Oh, that's the drugs," the medical person pooh-poohed dismissively.

"No, it's not the drugs. I can assure you of that. My dad is dying," I said very firmly, and walked away, knowing there was no point in continuing the discussion.

It was a young nurse who insisted that Dad's consultant be called for a family meeting, the following day, because she wanted to know what procedures to follow if my dad went into cardiac arrest and he had to be resuscitated. The electric shocks would be painful, she told us, and it would just prolong his trauma for a few days more.

She knew exactly what was happening, even if she wasn't allowed to say so. Nurses always know, because they are so familiar with their patients. In her gentle, loving way, she said in so many words what we already knew, and her insistence on the consultant being called was why my dad's passing was so gentle and painless. We, as a family, are so much in her debt: her firm stance changed my dad's care from medical to palliative, enabling him to slip away to my mother's loving arms.

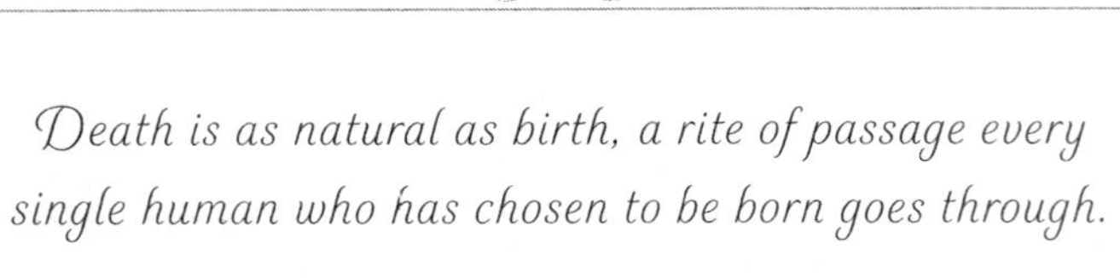

Death is as natural as birth, a rite of passage every single human who has chosen to be born goes through.

I remembered reading Dr Elisabeth Kübler-Ross's *On Death and Dying*, many years ago, when she wrote of how many in the medical profession feel that they have failed when their patients die. But death is as natural as birth, a rite of passage every single human who has chosen to be born goes through.

Doctors and medical personnel do not always know best, even though they feel they are doing their best and have given wonderful medical attention to the patient. But death is a reality, and the Spirit and body know what to do to prepare.

We stopped trying to get Dad to eat, to make us feel better, when he didn't want to. We tried to respect and accommodate every step he took along the path of his leaving.

I'm crying as I write, remembering how hard it was to let go because we so dearly loved him and my mother. But sometimes the letting go is the most loving thing you can ever do for the ones you love most. The knowledge that my brothers, sister and I made it as easy as we could for Dad to go peacefully, without anxiety or stress, gives us great comfort now.

If you are caring for a terminally ill loved one, and you've never had the experience of being with someone who is preparing to die, this is advice I would share from my personal experience in this area.

- Always try to follow their lead.

- Don't force them to try and eat or do what they no longer wish to do, such as reading the paper or watching TV.

- Be gentle, accepting and accommodating to ensure that their journey is not fraught with arguments, even with the best of intentions.

- Don't shy away from letting the person give away their belongings or make their funeral plan if they want to. But don't force the conversation if they are reluctant to pursue it. Both my parents had specific items and jewellery that they wanted each of us to have. They told us who was to have what, and it was a comfort to them and us, knowing that something very special to them was given to each of us as a bequest.

- It's very important to honour their choices. It will also be a great help in the aftermath of their death. It's very hard but ultimately you will be glad to have gone down this road: you will look back and know you did your very best for your loved one when they were at their most vulnerable.

- Relatives and those who assist in the care of the dying are used to seeing certain end-of-life signs, which offer us insight into the Spiritual and emotional changes taking place in the person who is facing death. Subtle changes may take place months before death occurs as the body prepares to shut down and the soul prepares to take the next step on its journey.

- The individual may experience all, some or perhaps none, but it's helpful to know what may lie ahead. Having seen my mother's passing, I was much more prepared when it came to assisting my dad on his journey. My older cousins, and friends like Aidan, Pam and Mary Helen, who had all been down that route, gave me invaluable advice, as indeed had my dear mother, when she was alive. This is why talking to people about death, becoming "intimate" with death, can be so helpful. It takes away the fear of the unknown and helps you to prepare for what lies ahead.

Below we have put together information gathered from our studies into the process of dying, and our collective personal experiences tending to loved ones at the time of death. They are not set in stone—for dying is as individual to each person as living is. But they are general guidelines to help understand what might be expected, which can bring a degree of comfort and alleviate fears at this difficult time.

These pertain to the death process of someone who has been ill or is nearing the end of life through old age.

The Early Stages of Death

- The person may begin to "withdraw" from all they previously found enjoyable, such as watching TV or reading. They may not be as chatty as they once were.

- They may want to talk about dying. Don't change the subject: be guided by them and be honest with them. It's a very natural conversation to have and is so helpful to you and them.

- They will begin to eat and drink much less as the body prepares for its final task of shutting down. Give them smaller portions, and let them eat little and often. If they refuse food, don't force them or make a big issue of eating.

- The person may complain of being cold, and may be cool to the touch. Make sure to keep them warm.

- They may sleep a lot, especially in the daytime. During this time of sleeping they are often between worlds, becoming used to the other side. Aidan had advised me of this, and I knew when Dad started sleeping for long periods in the afternoons that it was a sign of what was coming.

- The colour of the skin may change. The eyes will become dimmer, losing their sparkle as the life force slowly begins to ebb away. Sometimes they seem to be looking into the distance, lost in thought, and seem to be unaware of your presence.

- They may say they have spoken to people who are already dead, or that they have been to places or seen things not visible to you. Don't contradict them or try to explain anything away as a hallucination or drug reaction. Be reassuring and affirming of their experience.

- My mother told me she kept seeing her mother, and this was two weeks before she went into hospital; she was not taking any drugs at the time. My dad was still sharp and aware when he told me both his parents were with him, sitting at the side of his bed. He found it very comforting, he added, and I was so glad he wasn't disturbed by seeing his parents, who had come through from beyond the veil. My godmother, who was in a nursing home and not on heavy drugs, told me her sister, who had passed many years previously, had cut her hair for her when I complimented her on how nice it was.

- Affirm those visions. If your loved one is disturbed by them—although most won't be—reassure them that it's normal and natural: say, "Yes, these things happen. It's okay. There's nothing to fear." Reassurance is everything.

Nearing the End

- As death becomes more imminent and the person may be bedbound or sitting in their chair, they will sleep even more and become confused when awake, perhaps not knowing the time, day or place when they wake up.

- My dad's last lucid words to me were, "What time is it? Were you called in?" I told him it was ten past one during the day, and that it was visiting time, although I had been with him all morning. That reassured him and he drifted off to sleep again.

- Incontinence of bladder and bowel may set in. If the person is in a hospital, hospice or nursing home, it will be taken care of. If at home, the health nurse or palliative care nurse will advise and assist you, if you have engaged their services. There is always help at hand if you ask for it. Your doctor or healthcare professional will tell you who to contact.

- The person may be drowsy or confused. Tell them who you are, explain things to them, if necessary: "The doctor's here to have a look at you'; "It's time to take your tablets'; "I'll help you have a wash."

- Occasionally, someone close to death may rally and have a short-lived increase in energy and alertness. This is known as "the surge." They may become talkative after a period of sleepiness. They may want to eat a favourite food. They may choose to see visitors after a period of withdrawal and be eager to talk. Take advantage of this time because it can be one of special intimacy, a last chance to express your love and support.

Occasionally, someone close to death may rally and have a short-lived increase in energy and alertness. This is known as "the surge."

Imminent Death

There are numerous signs that death may be imminent.

- The person may start plucking at the bedclothes or their clothing and become restless. I remember my mother telling me this was a sign death was near when her own sisters died, and when I saw her do it I knew it wouldn't be long. Don't try to prevent or restrain these movements.
- Speak in a calm, reassuring way to the person: tell them you're with them and there's nothing to worry about.
- Play soft music if you think it would help, or say some prayers with them if they have a faith or religion.
- Stroke their arm or hand in a comforting manner if you think this will help.
- The "death rattle." This ominous term comes from a gurgling sound inside the chest, as the person is in the last stage of dying. It doesn't indicate pain and is simply part of the physical process of dying. Turn their head to the side to

drain secretions and wipe their mouth with a moist cloth.

- Small chips of ice or frozen juice will help keep their mouth from becoming dry.

- Breathing will change. The person may take shallow breaths with periods of no breathing for a few seconds and up to a minute. There may be periods of rapid, shallow panting. Elevating their head or turning them on their side may bring relief.

It can be very hard not to sob as you watch a loved one fading away from you. But save the weeping for when you are in a private space. The dying person needs to be completely focused on their last Earthly experience and undertaking. Instead, reassure them, give them permission to go and know this is the most generous and loving thing you can do for them.

Don't distress them if possible but do say your goodbyes and tell them, if it's the case, how much you love them. If you have an apology to make, make it and release both of you from whatever blocked your relationship.

Remember that if it's not right for the person to have you or anyone else there when they die, that's fine. It's not a failing on anyone's part. As Mary Helen's experience with her much-loved dad which she describes later shows, he needed to be on his own to pass.

As you will see in Mary Helen's segment "Healing the Family Tree," at a Spiritual level the soul knows how, when and where it will depart, even if on the Earthly plane people think they may not be prepared.

They may, like the friend she writes about, make declarations or requests that seem out of character. Sometimes they want to see if you are ready to let go. If the person wants to be alone or with someone else, it doesn't mean they don't love you or that you aren't important to them. They are just finding the easiest way to die, and that's all right. Remember, we, too, will be in that position when our time comes.

All that is important to remember is that we should assist the dying person to leave this Earth as gently and lovingly as possible in the months, weeks, days and hours coming up to their departure.

At a Spiritual level the soul knows how, when and where it will depart, even if on the Earthly plane people think they may not be prepared.

Aidan

During the last weeks of my mam's life I could see signs that she was preparing to go, just as Tricia has written about. The sleeping, not eating and uneasiness in her were all confirmation to me that she was between the two worlds. Mam was also happy to see her loved ones who had passed.

My niece Tine had come home from Denmark to see her nanny. She was a nurse and had also worked in a senior citizens' home for a time during her training. She was great with Mam, as she understood the process of dying and how to deal with it. On her last visit she had pointed out that

Mam's nose was starting to go slightly to one side, a sign that death is coming, and to keep an eye on it. As people approach their final days and hours before death, circulation can decrease, especially in the elderly. The first areas to be affected are the extremities, such as fingertips, toes, ears and the nose. The tip can become necrotic, where the tissue begins to die due to lack of blood and oxygen. Not only can it change colour, but it may lose its firmness and shape, giving the appearance of "crooking" to one side.

I remember telling Tricia this when her dad was preparing to pass, and she told me her sister had remarked on the change in their dad's nose that very day. During Mam's last weeks I began to notice this more and more. I remember sitting on the bed with her one morning, helping her to dress, when she said to me, "I think my time is near. My feet are very hot. I felt them this morning. I know that feeling."

"What does that mean, Mam?" I asked.

"When I was looking after the old people, their feet always got warm before they died, a burny warm."

"Are you ready to die?" I asked her.

"Yes, son. There comes a time when we're all ready to go," she assured me.

My heart was breaking but I didn't let her know. I gave her a hug and told her how much I loved her.

As I held Mam's hand two weeks later in hospital, I noticed a change in her breathing. A young male nurse came in, checked her and told us very lovingly that, yes, her breathing had changed and she had about half an hour left, so if we wanted to call anyone in they needed to come quickly.

He was correct. She went peacefully within the half-hour with most of her family around her. She had a beautiful death, which made me even less afraid of dying.

A Message from a Palliative Care Worker

A young woman named Corry had come to me for healing when I was working in Holland. She is from Belgium and we struck up a friendship right away. There was something unique about her energy when she walked into the room: I could see that she worked with people in a very special way and helped them on the last stage of their soul journey. When she told me what she did I was very taken by the love she had for her "guests," as she called them.

Here are some questions I asked her about caring for the dying.

> *Tell me about where you work, Corry.*
>
> I work in a palliative day care centre, Aidan. It's a place for people who are terminally ill. Our guests are very ill but still able to live at home. They regularly come to our day centre so we can care for them. Although they can't be cured they still have some time left here on Earth. Sometimes it's only weeks or even days, but during this time we're there for them and look after them as much as possible.
>
> *What are the main goals of the centre?*
>
> The two main goals of our centre are:
>
> 1. Providing care for our guests and giving them a nice relaxing day in every possible way.

2. Providing respite for their carers, who are often forgotten.

Those two goals together make it possible for our guests to remain at home for as long as they can and as long as they want to be there.

What kind of care do you provide for your guests?

Our care takes place on all levels, physical, psychological, social and Spiritual. We try to meet every possible desire our guests may have. Although we cannot take away the illness or the sorrow they are carrying, we stand by them and support them every step of the way. We act with the deepest respect for the person and the process they are going through.

We have a lot of tools we use to give them the best care possible. We can take away most of the physical pain, comfort them, pamper them, give psychological support, or just simply have a long talk with them. We are there for them at all times. We support, encourage, and walk next to them at their own pace, listening and adjusting to their needs and desires.

What do you think works best for your guests?

It is the warmth, friendship and love that the team have for each other, which extends to the guests and their carers, that is the true strength of our centre. It is this love that reaches everyone's heart, opening it slowly in a wonderful and beautiful

way. That love gives our guests confidence, and strength at this difficult and traumatic time.
This supportive energy helps our guests to gain back some happiness and joy in their lives, which are otherwise so controlled by their illnesses.

Nothing is more touching and beautiful for us than to see their hearts open again, being able to enjoy the little things in life, to come to a place of acceptance and peace.

In my opinion, love and respect are the principal strengths during this transition period. It is what helps our guests come to terms with themselves, their illnesses and their deaths. This happens at the patient's own pace. Doing our work with great respect, love and understanding makes such a difference to the healing of everyone concerned.

Can you tell us a little about your guests?

I will never forget John. John had ALS [motor neurone disease] and when he came to us, he was in great need of care in every way you can imagine.

He couldn't move his arms, legs or body, and had to communicate by using a special computer operated by a laser connected to his glasses. The only mobility he had was to move his head slightly. He had also lost his ability to speak. The first week he came to us his daughter was with him. She explained to us what he needed and how everything had to be done. For him, it was crucial that we took care of him as he wanted. We understood that: it was one of the only things left for him to control.

In my opinion, love and respect are the principal strengths during this transition period. It is what helps our guests come to terms with themselves, their illnesses and their deaths.

I remember thinking, Oh, my God, how are we ever going to provide him with all the care he needs? His needs were many and complicated but it was very touching to see the love and the patience with which his daughter helped and supported him. She was one of the many unsung heroes who care for their loved one at home.

Within a week, John had stolen everyone's heart with his smile and his unparalleled humour. We all loved him and he accepted and loved us back. This mutual love and respect made it possible for him to trust us and at the same time gave us the confidence to take care of him. It created a very special bond between us.

He enjoyed being with us and we enjoyed caring for him. I find it difficult to describe how special John was. He was pure love. He joined us on our annual holiday to the coast, and I will never forget the smile on his face every morning when we came to wake him up. That smile was on his face even while he slept.

In the end, he couldn't communicate using his computer any more. He could only use his eyes and his heart. But the love and trust we had built up over the previous months made it possible to understand him. From heart to heart, from soul to soul, in love and through love we understood everything.

What is the best thing about your job?

Taking care of our guests is sometimes hard, especially when it is time to let them go. But nothing can compete with the beautiful gift of love we receive each day. It brings you back to what life is all about. Our guests' strength, courage, beauty, and way of living are an example to every one of us.

Their friendship and joy are heart-warming; this is the gift they offer me every single day. I ask myself, How can someone so close to death give me so much? Then I realise: they are so near God and His wonderful light, they are at peace. Standing next to them every day is indeed a great honour.

The Hospice Prayer

O' gracious God, Giver of all hope and comfort,
You have called us here to be the companions
of those who are making their way home.
As you draw them into your healing light, touch us also.
Transform our knowledge into vision, our skill into comfort,
our pain into compassion and our grief into love;
That those who go before us may leave in dignity and peace,
and that we may grow in gratitude.
Amen.

"Death is nothing else but
going home to God, the
bond of love will be
unbroken for all eternity."

—Mother Teresa

Facing Fear of Death

Fear of death is as natural as life itself. It is part of being human. But it is also something that can be much alleviated, when we recognise it and allow it to be part of our lives, rather than trying to push it away. To become intimate with death, we must acknowledge our fear of it, and only then can we make friends with it. Here Aidan describes his relationship with it, and what the angels have assured him awaits, on the other side.

Aidan

I don't want to die but I don't fear dying. I suppose, like most people, my greatest fear is not in dying but the manner in which I depart this life. My wish is to die in my sleep and feel no pain. To jump on that bus when it comes and let it take me to my final destination. That place of light and love to be reunited with my loved ones in my heavenly home. To be in the presence of God and feel his unconditional love. Party time, I call it.

I don't know many people who want to die, unless they are in really bad pain, either physically or emotionally. In my line of work, I come across those who fear what will happen to them when they pass over. Many still hold on to the old ways of thinking, that we will be judged not for all the good things we did in life but for the mistakes we made, for our "sins."

My angels explained this to me beautifully. We do not commit sins, but we do make mistakes, and we must learn from our mistakes, or similar situations keep repeating until we do.

That terrible four-letter word makes many of us suffer in fear and guilt during life, and in our dying often holds us back from embracing the wonderful light that is God; the God who loves us unconditionally in life and in death.

My angels explained this to me beautifully. We do not commit sins, but we do make mistakes, and we must learn from our mistakes, or similar situations keep repeating until we do.

Once we learn from them, we break the cycle, and we will never make the same mistake again. This enriches our lives and enables us to grow Spiritually. If we don't learn from our mistakes, and continue to close our eyes to the hurts we cause people (and ourselves), we will feel less connected to God, which will make our lives more difficult and unfulfilled.

God does not judge or punish us. God's love is unconditional. It is humans who judge, and try to control or bully. When things go wrong, and we have no answers, it's easy to lash out at God—but the real answer lies in man's free will or ego.

You can change your path in life, and usually struggle with it, but in most cases you return to the soul plan. That's where we find happiness and contentment. People may be very successful but unfulfilled in their careers, so they change to do what they were always meant to do. Tricia and I, for example, took a huge leap of faith to leave the security of our permanent pensionable jobs to do what we love doing and follow our soul purpose and plan.

If something is pushing at you, listen to your inner voice and make the change that is calling out to be made.

Sister Ann's Story

I will share with you a lovely experience I had with one of my clients on the subject of dying and her fear of the other side. This person was a nun in her mid-eighties—we'll call her Sister Ann—and she had been in holy orders for at least six decades. Sister Ann had come to me for many years, and I really looked forward to her visits. I'd make sure to put her in for my last appointment as our sessions always ran over time. I thoroughly enjoyed her stories and wisdom, which she freely shared. I learned so much from her.

Sister Ann had a wicked sense of humour and we laughed a lot. We also shared a belief in God and His angels, and how they had helped us in our lives.

Ann started coming to me when she felt hurt and let down by the Church. She felt guilty for all the wrong it had done to so many people. At this time, she had also begun to look at the Spiritual side of her life as opposed to the religious side. She felt the religious side had too many rules and was very restrictive, not allowing her to think for herself.

She had entered the convent when she was in her late teens, and from that day she was told how to think, dress, speak and even what and when to eat. She felt she had no free will and now, in the last stages of her life, was enjoying a new relationship with God, finding "a peaceful way," as she put it, to be with Him, seeing things in a much simpler way. "No rules," she would tell me. "I'm free to think for myself and see God in everything and everybody."

One day, she asked me, "Will God forgive me for standing by and allowing these things to happen? How will I ever explain it to Him?"

I was so surprised at this question coming from such a beautiful soul. "You?" I replied. "Why would you of all people ask this question, Ann? You who glow because there is so much love inside you, and you who have so many people around you who love you so much that, even to this day, ex-students are still calling you and taking you to lunch. You have nothing to fear. God will be so happy to see you come. He already has your seat waiting."

"I do hope so," was all she said.

The sparkle in her eyes faded a little and her energy weakened. "How could the Church get it so wrong? How could they do this to us?"

"This is not for you to worry about," I told her. "You got it right, Ann, and that's all you have to remember."

She gave me an uncertain smile. We talked for a while longer and then she said she had to go.

As always, I helped her with her coat and gave her a hug, but I could see that she was troubled. The smile had disappeared from her eyes.

"Are you okay, Ann?" I asked.

She looked at me, and her face turned red. "I need to ask you something and I feel a bit silly," she said.

"Ask away," I urged, anxious to get to the root of her concerns.

"When we die what happens to us?" she asked hesitantly. I was taken aback, not by the question but from whom it had come.

I looked at her for a few seconds, then said, "I can only tell you what the angels told me and I hope this will help you. We never die alone. Our loved ones and the angels are always with us at the end."

My angel Hannah had told me, "There is nothing to be afraid of in death. You will be prepared for your crossing. For a period of time before you cross over, your Spirit and soul travel to Heaven, so you can adjust to this new energy. Here in this great light you become reacquainted with your loved ones who have already passed and you will become steadily attuned to the lighter God energy to which you have travelled. You will become a child of both worlds for this blessed time, and this is why so many very ill people speak of, and even see, loved ones who have passed, before they themselves journey to the light of eternal love and peace."

I smiled at my dear friend. "You *know* this, Ann. You have sat with many of your sisters in their moments of death. You have told me yourself about the joy you experienced in helping them in their last days, how they told you about seeing their family members and how happy this made them, what great comfort they took from seeing their loved ones again, and how it took all fear away from them. Hannah told me also not to be afraid of death, for beyond this Earth awaits a beautiful place of perfect peace. This is a place of reunion, as you already know. Here you are not judged by what you did or didn't do on Earth but are asked what you have learned. Life is a path of learning and we all choose to learn certain lessons in life. The God who creates you loves you with unconditional love. Unconditional love doesn't judge or condemn.

My angel Hannah had told me, "There is nothing to be afraid of in death. You will be prepared for your crossing."

"You have nothing to fear, only fear itself. Your crossing will be perfect and joyous, and they will all be there to meet and greet you," I promised her.

"That's it?" she said. "There's no punishment?"

"No! Just peace and love."

"So, it's not sitting in front of God for eternity, singing His praises and worshipping Him?" she asked, in an almost childlike manner.

"No," I assured her. "Not at all."

"Thank God! I spent one lifetime doing that and I don't want to spend eternity doing the same." She laughed, but I could see the relief in her face.

As I hugged her I knew in my heart that she was ready to move on. She took my hand and said, "Thank you, dear Aidan. I feel so light and happy now. You have put my heart at rest." Her glow had returned, along with her cheeky smile. "Sleep well, dear friend," she said, waving gaily as she left.

That was the last time I saw Sister Ann alive, but I do know she passed peacefully in the absolute knowledge that she was truly loved by God, the God to whom she had dedicated her entire life with such wholehearted gentleness, conscientiousness and purity.

If people truly knew what awaits them when they "die," a burden would be lifted from mankind's shoulders, as it was lifted from Ann's, and people would live differently, without fear.

Mary Helen

I'd like to talk a little about how our own approach to our death can impact not only on our own experience of it, but also on the experiences of those around us, our loved ones, who are so sad to see us go.

In the following piece, I'll draw out, with the blessing of those involved, how the attitude of the person who is dying can shape how those of us who are left behind can not alone cope through our grieving, but maintain a real and vibrant connection to our lost loved one, in the aftermath.

This is the story of a very dear soul friend, Kate. Sadly, Kate—a former solicitor turned angel healer—is no stranger to loss and death. Her husband passed after a relatively short bout of cancer in 2004. Devastation struck when, in December 2012, Kate's only son Alan died suddenly. He was a vibrant, healthy and wonderful young man, and his death shook our community to its core.

Kate's brother Dick had been unable to attend his nephew's funeral because he had been diagnosed with an aggressive cancer earlier in the year. His chemotherapy prevented him making the trip from England to be with his family in Ireland, but he was constantly texting and emailing words of comfort.

Everyone was affected by the way Dick handled his imminent death. As his wife said in an email to Kate in the aftermath, "He was so brave and dealt with his illness in an amazing way, with humour and dignity. It was just so sad that he had to leave us." Kate added that not once during his illness or after Kate's son had passed did Dick ever have a case of poor-me. In fact, as death drew closer, Dick would write beautiful texts to his family, trying to ease their pain by showing them he didn't fear death and neither should they.

Dick wrote to Kate after she shared a poem her daughter Anna had been given in a counselling session. "She Is Gone" by David Harkins eloquently expresses the possibilities of light and darkness that can come after loss, and how the choice we make can impact fundamentally on how we fare—whether to cry at the loss, or to smile for what we had.

Thanks, Sis!

THAT'S the formula to finding the answers on how to cope. Absolutely wonderful that it's not some religious claptrap about the Pearly Gates, but a loving and practical road map for emotions which have been shot to pieces.

I told Kay to keep this, and USE it when I go. The bottom line is we are all going at some point or another, we're all moving closer to it every day. As Mum used to say to us, "They're coming and going all the time." Those who loved us, and go before us, do NOT want us suffering, no more than you or I will want to see intense suffering after we pass on. It'll only upset us and hold us back. I doubt if we can "move on" successfully if Earthly emotions are causing us deep unrest. Once we know our loved ones have accepted death as a natural process in the Great Scheme of things, we can begin the next stage of our "journey" in peace. So try and "smile because he has lived." FORTUNATELY in our circle, Alan could have been given to others! Instead WE got him and HOW LUCKY for us . . . and similarly, how lucky for him. With you as his mother and Anna his sister, it was a win/win partnership!!! And always remember it as that, not a win/lose partnership. Love is not something that passes when we do, it remains with us forever . . .

And you were RIGHT when you said to Anna, "We WILL get through this." . .

MUCH LOVE n HUGS Xxxxxxxxxxxxx

Dick

Of course it is important to mention that while some who prepare to pass are seemingly together and well-adjusted to the idea, others may be terrified to leave or go through the actual death process. They may put on a brave face but not everyone has the conviction of Kate's brother Dick that all will be fine.

Often, the dying spend more time trying to comfort those who will be left behind than concentrating on dying well. Sometimes the grieving forget to think about the emotional needs of the one who is actually preparing to pass.

Dick and his positive texts about death really held things together for his family. It is remarkable to find someone who knows at the core of his being that there is nothing to fear and spends his last days showering the people he loved with his messages of faith, courage and love. To see his legacy passed on to you would have pleased him no end. This is a beautiful example of how the souls of our loved ones leave footprints on our hearts, and never truly leave us.

Affirmation for Facing Fear of Death

Higher power
In your great mercy, I ask that you
set me free from my fear of death
For there is nothing to fear in a journey
back to a place called home
Nothing to fear in entering the light of love
I place my trust in You to look after those I leave behind,
and hold them in your unending love and care
For I am only a heartbeat away, there when they call out
my name, until we meet again in the place of one Love.

"No man is my friend, no man is my enemy, every man is my teacher."

—from *The Game of Life*
by Florence Scovel Shinn

The Grieving Process and the Gifts Death Brings

Patricia

Throughout life, grief comes to us all in many forms. It may be for the ending of a relationship, the loss of good health, a home, a job or career, financial security or a loved one through death. Everyone will experience grief differently and in different stages.

Sometimes we are given time to prepare for the loss of the loved one. At other times, death is sudden, unexpected, tragic, and a numbing sense of shock can be even stronger than the grief, which will come later.

Initially, in those surreal days after a death, we are taken up with practicalities. Relatives and friends have to be notified. A funeral has to be organised. In a way, these distractions are a blessing. They give us time to absorb the enormity of what has befallen us. They give us a chance to do our best for our loved one in the tasks we have to undertake for them: our last gift of service.

I remember going into the undertaker's with my dad and siblings after my mother's death. I had passed that building thousands of times and never given it a thought. Now, unthinkably, we were seated with a most compassionate and understanding undertaker, handing the burden of arrangements over to him,. being guided on every step that had to be taken. There were moments of humour when we looked at the array of coffins, knowing instinctively that my mother would not have liked the rather flashy, ornate ones.

Later, I remember going into my local supermarket and hearing two people laughing. How can they laugh? I thought. How can the world just keep on as though nothing has happened? My mother is *dead*!

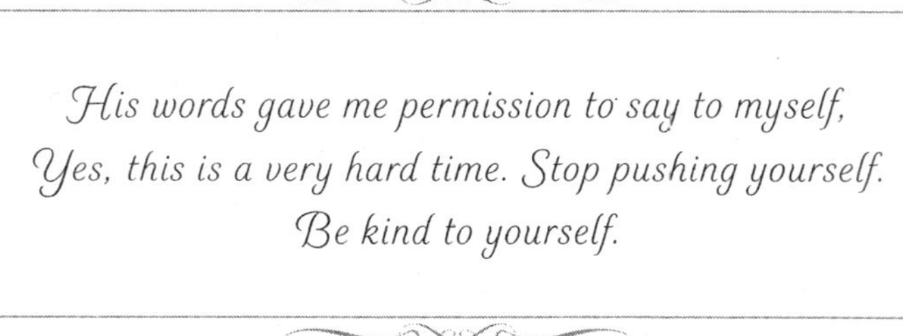

I remember the awfulness of actually saying those words to someone for the first time. "My mother has died!" I could hardly believe it, even though I had been at her bedside. It's strange what you remember about those days.

I remember being in the funeral car. How many times had I blessed myself and said a prayer, as is the custom in Ireland, every time a funeral cortège passed? Had I ever thought I would be a mourner one day watching people bless themselves as we drove by? I remember being touched as we drove past by the sight of a young man, selling newspapers at traffic lights, removing his baseball cap and bowing as he made the sign of the cross. That simple, heartfelt moment of a stranger's kindness will stay with me always.

I remember friends, acquaintances and neighbours standing with us in solidarity at the funeral mass and the wake, sometimes just pressing our hands or hugging wordlessly. Such kindness. Such comfort.

I remember a couple of months after my mother died, a lovely photographer, who had taken publicity shots of me, arranging to work on the photo of my mother that we had chosen for her memory card. As he was leaving, he said to me, "This is a very, very hard time. Be good to yourself."

Somehow, it was a shock to hear him say it. There had been so much to do. We had all rallied around my father and he had become our focus. I had to continue writing the novel I was in the middle of when my mother had passed—the reins of life had to be taken up again—and I hadn't really had time to realise that my mother's death was the hardest thing I had ever endured. His words gave me permission to say to myself, Yes, this is a very hard time. Stop pushing yourself. Be kind to yourself.

Sometimes it isn't that easy. One of my dearest friends, who had suffered the sudden loss of a brother, said to me a few days after my mother passed that waves of exhaustion would hit me out of the blue. She told me to be careful of my driving, to try to concentrate because invariably my thoughts would revert to the bedside vigil and the moments of passing. This was so true. Sometimes it was all I could think about, especially when driving. Then my mind would wander back.

Another friend offered me Xanax tablets and I was tempted to take them, but instinctively I knew it was not for me, though many people find it helpful to take medication at such times. I realised that grief had to be endured, no matter how long it was postponed, and I thought, I might as well deal with it now rather than later. Grief will have its way and has to be worked through, as does the anger, the depression, the sense of isolation, the guilt one invariably feels, remembering rows or disagreements that may have occurred or that you felt you hadn't done enough for your loved one when they were alive—even though you had.

During this period other questions often arise. "Is this it? Do we live whatever sort of life we live, and then just die? Is there a purpose to living or is it all very random?" As Pam explains further on, death can be a "great awakener" for those who are left, and those who mourn. Why? Where? How? So many questions.

Sometimes you may feel angry with the person who has passed because there were difficulties in your relationship with them. There may be no grief at all, just resentment. This is a hard path to walk.

Many years ago I opened a cherished book *The Game of Life* by Florence Scovel Shinn on the page with the quote at the chapter beginning: "No man is my friend, no man is my enemy, every man is my teacher."

At that time, my world view was beginning to change, and I found it to be such an interesting concept. It changed my view of relationships with family, friends, and partners.

There are people we don't get on with in our lifetime and that's fine. It would be a perfect world if the opposite were true. But if you ask yourself, What is that person teaching me, or what am I teaching them? the answer may bring a different energy to the association.

It may be a parent, sibling, child, partner, friend, or workmate who has been in our life for a specific reason. And when their death occurs and there is estrangement, one is left with the distress of knowing that nothing has been resolved, closure never achieved.

If you are in a difficult situation like this, there is an affirmation that can be very helpful. Simply say:

> *I put my problems, regrets, anger and resentment with [name] in the hands of Divine wisdom and love, release it to the Universe, and go free.*

Say it when all the emotions come surging up, and believe that in time a healing balm will come and you may even be able to bless the one who troubled you.

Share memories, especially of good times, but don't push any difficulties you had under the carpet. No relationship is perfect, no shared life is without its challenges. Acknowledge them and let them go.

However grief assails you, it's important to remember that help in the form of counselling or therapy is available, if you feel you need it. This can be a positive step in your self-care at this vulnerable time. It's also important to make the most of family and friends. Sometimes sitting down with them over a cuppa and chatting about the person who has passed is extremely therapeutic.

Share memories, especially of good times, but don't push any difficulties you had under the carpet. No relationship is perfect, no shared life is without its challenges. Acknowledge them and let them go.

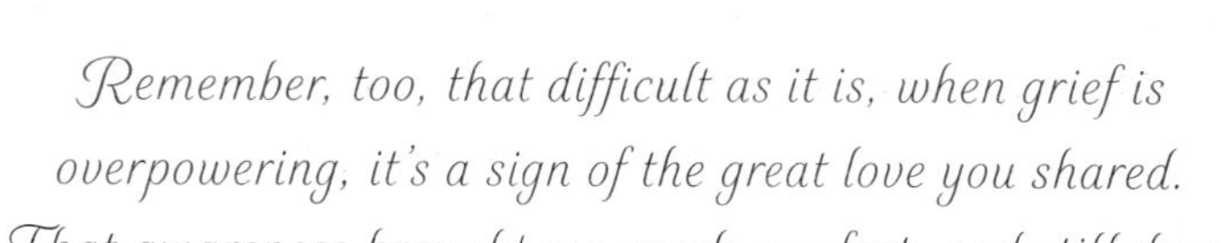

Remember, too, that difficult as it is, when grief is overpowering, it's a sign of the great love you shared. That awareness brought me much comfort, and still does.

A wise friend of mine once told me that grief is like a tsunami at first—overwhelming and unstoppable—but that in time the waves lessen and grow calmer until, over many years, they are merely ripples. I didn't believe her, although I wanted to, in the throes of devastation when my mother passed away. Years later I realise she was right, and as I now grieve my father's death, I know that, in time, that grief, too, will lap gently on the shore.

Remember, too, that difficult as it is, when grief is overpowering, it's a sign of the great love you shared. That awareness brought me much comfort, and still does.

I had the pleasure and privilege of meeting Aidan's wonderful mother, Kathleen. She had a terrific sense of humour. I remember having lunch with them one day. Aidan and I were working on our respective books and talking about our progress. After lunch Kathleen stood up and said, "Well, I don't have time to stay here gabbing, like you two. I'm going to my office." She walked out to the sunny conservatory and sat down at her sewing machine with a huge grin.

When Kathleen died, Aidan was naturally devastated, and he describes here how even his angelic gifts and knowledge of life beyond the veil did not prevent his deep sense of bereavement.

Because my mother had died six months before Aidan's, I understood the stages of grief he was passing through and was able to reassure him that all he was experiencing was very natural. But it took time before his sense of connection to the spirit world was restored, as he discusses here.

Aidan

Now is your time of grief, but I will see you again and you will rejoice and no one will take away your joy. —John 16:22

There is no right or wrong way to go about grieving—it is as personal as any other aspect of our individuality. Sometimes it is immediate, and other times it is delayed, and can bubble up when least expected, with little or no forewarning. This often happens when the grief is buried at the time of death, and I have had clients come to me concerned that they are not experiencing grief in the way they think they should, or at all—as they feel a kind of emptiness, deadness or "nothingness" inside in the wake of loss.

There can be different reasons for this, and Tricia talks more on it below, but the important thing is to be assured that there is nothing wrong if this is the case. As the angels tell us, everything is unfolding as it should be, and with a greater purpose than we can often intuit, bound by our Earthly bodies and human ways.

My own experience of the loss of my beloved mother was of a heavy grief that had lasted for a solid year, and did not seem at the point of alleviation as I stood in my kitchen, feeling desolate, on the morning of her first anniversary—unaware of something unexpected just around the corner, which I'll speak more of later. At that moment, I thought about how people had told me it would get better after this time, but it didn't seem so. The intense pain of loss, which ebbed and flowed, felt as severe as ever—the knowledge that I would never again hear her voice, or experience one of her all-embracing hugs.

A year of grief. Never had I felt so hollow and empty. Her death had hit me hard. I felt trapped, alone and helpless, nothing mattered any more. I had cried myself to sleep on more than a few occasions. It was the worst time of my life. I tried to put on a brave face for people. I really wanted to talk to them about Mam, but I didn't know how so I stayed quiet. It was such a different experience of loss from what I'd felt when my father had died, which had in no way prepared me for the grief of losing my beloved mother.

A year of grief. Never had I felt so hollow and empty. Her death had hit me hard. I felt trapped, alone and helpless, nothing mattered any more. I had cried myself to sleep on more than a few occasions.

Thank God for Tricia and my friend Bo: I could always pour my heart out to them. They understood and could give me great advice and comfort.

"Time is a great healer," my friends and neighbours comforted me, and eventually I knew they were right.

Less helpful was when people told me I should be grateful I'd had Mam for so long and to let her go. The truth was that having had Mam with me for so long made it even worse. She had lived with me when everyone had married and moved away from home. She was part of the day-to-day fabric of my life.

Drinking my tea on her anniversary I could remember clearly every minute of my mother's last day on Earth. I had been working in Japan, giving talks and workshops, when she became ill. I remember the phone ringing in the middle of the night, in my hotel room, and hearing my nephew's voice saying words that were so hard to hear, "We all think it best you come home now."

I remember getting on the plane and the endless journey back to Ireland. I prayed the whole time, pleaded with God to keep Mam alive until I got there.

It was a mild December day when I landed in Dublin, and I went straight to the hospital. There, the family was gathered around her, just as she would have wished. Seeing her tired body breathing quietly, I was so relieved to have made it in time. She had not opened her eyes for more than twelve hours. The doctors and nurses were so kind and gentle with her, and with us.

"Did she want any intervention?" a doctor asked me.

"No." That wasn't easy to say because I wanted her to stay with me as long as possible. But we had talked about this before I'd left for Japan, and I was clear about her wishes.

The day before I'd left, she had asked me if there was a Hell. I told her no, and assured her that when she died, she would be embraced by a wonderful light and she would meet all her loved ones who had previously passed. There would be a big celebration. She told me she had seen most of her family already, over the past few weeks, but that she had not seen my dad yet and she was a bit worried about that. I told her he would be the one to take her hand and bring her safely to the other side. She was very happy to hear that.

She went on to tell me what kind of funeral she wanted, what she wanted to wear, the church she wanted her Mass said in and even some of the hymns and readings she'd like. She also informed me she wanted to be waked at home and didn't want to be put on "any of those machines to keep me alive. When God calls me I want to go without delay," she said.

The day before I'd left, she had asked me if there was a Hell. I told her no, and assured her that when she died, she would be embraced by a wonderful light and she would meet all her loved ones who had previously passed.

When He did call her, in the early hours of the following morning, she went with great peace and no pain. She had the most wonderful smile on her face, and I knew she was happy and safely home. An indescribable white and purple light surrounded her as she journeyed to the next life.

I remember coming home from the funeral a few days later, with my friend Bo, and feeling how lonely, cold and empty the house was. Bo had lost both her parents and I asked her if it got easier, or if you ever stopped missing the hugs. I knew she would give me an honest answer. I still remember her powerful words, and I thank her for them.

"You never stop missing them or missing the hugs, but it does get easier. You learn to live your life in a different way. The first year is a year of sadness and regrets but as time passes you learn to laugh again and think of all the good and happy times you had together."

"I can't imagine that, but I do want to believe you," I said.

"Well, did your mam cry and seem unhappy every time she spoke about her parents?"

"No. She laughed a lot when she mentioned them."

"I rest my case," said Bo.

And the unexpected thing that I mentioned at the beginning of this piece?

As I stood in the kitchen in desolation a year on from Mam's death, I heard something moving down the hall. The door opened into the kitchen, but nothing was there. Then I heard my mother saying, in her strong voice, "Enough is enough!" I knew she was telling me to get on with my life and stop holding myself back.

I always say there is no time limit on grief and everyone grieves in different ways and at their own pace—different strokes for different folks. Grief doesn't hold back the person who has died: the only one it holds back is the person who is grieving too much.

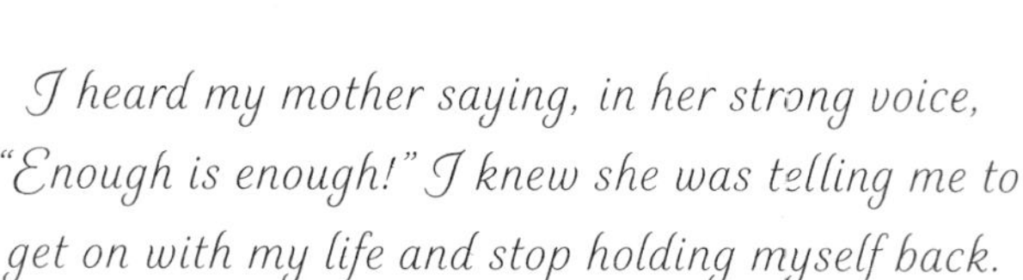

I heard my mother saying, in her strong voice, "Enough is enough!" I knew she was telling me to get on with my life and stop holding myself back.

If you are grieving, be gentle with yourself. Some grieve by filling their lives with things to do; others step away from socialising and going places, preferring to grieve in solitude. Whatever is right for you is what you must do, but a day will come when it's time to move on. Remember my mother's wise words: "Enough is enough." Life has to be lived and the last thing our loved ones would want is to let them hold us back from, as Tricia says, "opening the next chapter in our book of life."

I asked the angels for an affirmation for you in your grieving process, whatever shape it is taking, and this is what they delivered:

Affirmation from the Angels

I call upon my Guardian Angels to embrace me in their healing light and help me release all my feelings of pain, of sorrow and of grief. I give thanks for the love and happiness I shared with [insert name]. I let go and let God in, knowing that the bonds of love never die.

Patricia

Acknowledgement, Forgiveness and Healing

Death can bring the gift of healing and forgiveness, as Aidan will later show us as he describes the death of his father, with whom he had a difficult relationship throughout his life.

Aidan has also learned to forgive his sexual abuser, who died having not been brought to Earthly justice for his heinous crimes against children, a long and difficult process he describes in detail in his autobiography, *Angels of Divine Light*, where, ultimately, he went from being a "victim" to being "victorious."

As he describes it, "By holding on to unforgiveness we are still allowing the abuser to control our life. Don't give them this power, even from beyond the grave. By forgiving them we are setting ourselves free and telling them they have no power over us any more."

In the event of the death of someone towards whom you hold resentment and with whom you had unresolved issues, it is important not to bury the indescribable grief, rage, hate, anger, resentment and frustration that you have lived with. Engaging with, accepting and dealing with the emotions, bringing them to the surface to be faced and finally banished, is key.

I read once that denial of such a process is called "A Spiritual Bypass" and it's an apt description. "Oh, I've let it all go'; "Life's too short'; "I want to get on with my life." Those are some of the phrases we use to avoid facing the darkness within.

It is healing to honour and acknowledge the emotions of grief, rage, hate, anger, resentment and frustration, rather than to bury them deep or ignore them, where they will fester and can bring illness to your body. These are *your* wounds, but they are wounds that can be healed in time, if that is your intention. The choice is yours: we all have a choice in how we deal with the challenges (or lessons, if you prefer) life presents to us. "Victim." "Victorious."

Engaging with accepting and dealing with the emotions, bringing them to the surface to be faced and finally banished, is key.

While "forgiveness" is a wonderful gift, we cannot underestimate the trauma and devastation a person may be suffering because they have been left shattered and broken, unable to let go of what has happened to them, by the person who has passed on.

But rest assured, you have only to ask for Spiritual help and put the earnest intention out to the Universe that you *truly* want to forgive and move on, and help will be given to you in many ways.

As John O'Donohue writes so compassionately in *Eternal Echoes*, "When you forgive, some deeper, Divine generosity takes over. When you can forgive, then you are free. When you cannot forgive, you are a prisoner of the hurt done to you."

Carrying a grudge or holding on to anger, resentment or hatred do you far more damage than the person they are directed at, living or dead. They are the heaviest of life's burdens to bear. If you can find it in yourself to forgive, or let go, at some level, you will feel a lightness of Spirit and a sense of closure that can only bring a sense of welcome peace to you.

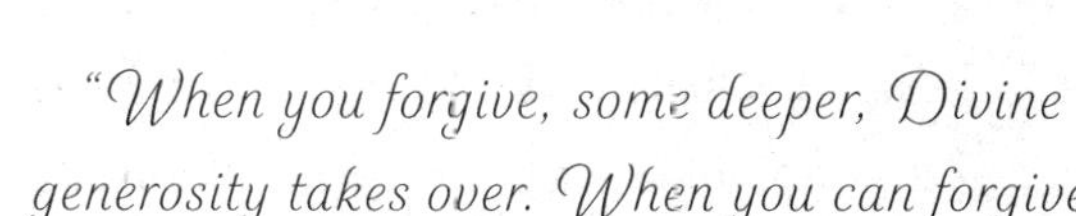

"When you forgive, some deeper, Divine generosity takes over. When you can forgive, then you are free. When you cannot forgive, you are a prisoner of the hurt done to you."

Pam will now introduce you to a powerful form of healing, both for you and the one who has crossed, *especially* if the relationship you had was difficult or abusive. Don't worry if you feel you can't do this: everything has its time, including forgiveness and forgiveness of self.

Pamela

Ho'oponopono: A Healing Gift in Life and Death

Ho'oponopono is based upon the Spiritual philosophy first used by Hawaiian tribal elders to mediate between people and their grievances to bring about forgiveness and a return to harmony.

It has since evolved into a modern-day healing modality through the work of Morrnah Simeona and Ihaleakala Hew Len. Meaning "to make right," it is now used by millions of people with the intention of cleansing and bringing peace and well-being into their lives.

Morrnah's mother was a sacred *kahuna lapa'au kahea*, one of the few remaining Hawaiian healers who used words and chants to heal. She trained her young daughter, and as Mornah grew and developed upon her own "path of divinity" she modified the original Ho'oponopono to include freedom from judgements for themselves, their relationships and their ancestry. At the age of seventy, Morrnah was honoured as a "Living Treasure of Hawaii" and in 1983 officially recognised as a *kahuna lapa'au kahea*, like her mother.

Dr Ihaleakala Hew Len was a student of Morrnah who became a Hawaiian healing master, teacher and therapist. He healed many patients with mental health issues by healing himself. Joe Vitlale and Hew Len have written about this in their book *Zero Limits*.

Hew Len tells us: "My job on Earth is twofold. My job is first of all to awaken people who might be asleep. Almost everyone is asleep. The only way I can awaken them is to work on myself." In death, as in life, grievances can reign. For those who've lost someone with whom they had a difficult or traumatic relationship, the wounds do not heal upon the person's passing. In fact, many buried feelings can come to the surface at this time. Perhaps a sense of anger or sadness that now there cannot be retribution for what was done to one may prevail; that the person will never be held to account. When old wounds reopen, healing may feel a long way off.

If this is true for you, this Hawaiian healing ritual may help. It is a healing modality of cleansing, but one for which you take full responsibility.

Hew Len has made many YouTube videos explaining the need to cleanse our thoughts (data) constantly and return to zero where we are in a state of "no-thing." In this heightened state of being, there is no-thing to forgive and we are clean of data, as we enter into a place of no-thought. But the silence of the soul takes practice.

Old wounds have a habit of reopening time and time again and we must be vigilant of our data/thoughts/baggage returning. Using the simple four statements of Ho'oponopono constantly in our lives is like doing yoga for the mind. The more we exercise our mind and become responsible for our thoughts and healing, the more we drop judgements, becoming lighter, fitter and more benign.

Ho'oponopono involves using four simple statements that are used to cleanse our mind and our relationships. They are: "I love you. I'm sorry. Please forgive me. Thank you."

Although the words are simple, and easy to chant, the concept is profound. I may have the knowledge that I am an instrument of light and an immense loving power but *being* it rather than *knowing* it is very different.

Unlike the days when priests and elders mediated for us with the Divine, we are now called upon to take full responsibility for healing everything in our lives and, significantly, in the world. Only we can do it for ourselves because we are now realising that we are the one and the whole. We share with every human the same potential for harm and peace.

"I love you. I'm sorry. Please forgive me. Thank you."

For many years I have heard my higher self reminding me: "All you have to do is to heal yourself and you heal the world." Saying "I love you. I'm sorry. Please forgive me. Thank you," mentally to others and to yourself whenever you become aware of tormented or judgemental thoughts, will help you cease the pattern of dis-eased thinking. Chanting in groups is powerful too. You may want to start your day with the intention to radiate Ho'oponopono into the world and your daily relationships. Anywhere, anytime, really. It is easy to forget so having the words on your mobile phone or computer may help. Cleansing our minds is a lifelong process.

Of course, that is all each of us has to do and it is simple but I have a powerful mind and a memory that reminds me of hurts and grievances, not only from my lifetime but also from my ancestral line. Although *I* may not be conscious of the bloodline affecting my mental state with dis-ease, it surely will.

I am, therefore, full of baggage and patterns of negative behaviours repeating over and over again in my life, disturbing me and others, as well as the equilibrium of human consciousness. The call for peace is awakening in us all on a mass scale and it begins inside ourselves.

We are aware that if we don't forgive, even though we feel justified in not doing so, we are continually contaminating our body and the world. There is a saying that "Resentment is like taking a poison and hoping it will harm the other person." It will, but we harm ourselves far more.

Thankfully, we are driven more powerfully by our innate Spiritual need for love, peace and harmony, devoid of torment. As well as dis-ease, my bloodline contains all the acts of loving kindness carried out by my kin and me.

Being aware of the duality inherent in the human condition is our greatest insight into realising we can rise above our little fearful "me" to open a place where our true self silently resides, awaiting our connection to knowing only oneness and unity. This is when we can observe human behaviours with understanding and love. In this higher state our only intention is to heal and to be at one. But we have to train our chattering mind first. This is when Ho'oponopono comes into its own too.

Start by looking at the behaviour of the person who has hurt you to such an extent you have been unable to forgive. It will probably be an abusive relationship that humiliated and diminished you. It will have made you feel small and disempowered. It may haunt you. You can never forgive because the person does not deserve forgiveness: they show no remorse.

Now, here is the crunch! Ho'oponopono asks you to take full responsibility for healing the situation, without blame or recriminations.

You are asked to look honestly into your life. Did *you* ever make anyone feel diminished even in a small way? If so, say the Ho'oponopono words to this person in your mind: "I love you. I'm sorry. Please forgive me. Thank you." Keep repeating these words until you feel cleansed. They are very powerful. Say them to yourself also. It is important not to project your pain back on to yourself. We are well practised in beating ourselves up and it is harmful, so keep up the words to your wounded self, too.

Say them to the television when you see children starving or people suffering the ravages of war. Send them to the person at the next table in the restaurant you overhear saying how they have been hurt because you will have hurt someone too. Empathy is a great Spiritual gift.

Everything you hear, see and experience is an opportunity for you to heal unconditionally.

It is important to make an intention to heal the blood running through your veins, from your ancestors, especially if the person you cannot forgive is of your blood family. In this way it removes you from attaching to the personal memory but it cleanses you both nevertheless.

Saying these simple words, "I love you. I'm sorry. Please forgive me. Thank you," has brought miraculous healing into many lives just because those people gave it a go, whether they believed in it or not.

Ho'oponopono is a powerful tool of healing that will lead us to enter the place where our silent observer resides, the silent space of pure awareness, beyond the torment, in us. In that moment, we experience a complete change of mind because we realise we are not our thoughts.

I have practised going within for many years to the point that I have eliminated many hurts and the need to blame. Of course, I am constantly given new situations that lower my vibration and I am there again with "How could they?" but now, mostly, I can quickly say, "I love you. Thank you for teaching me to get over myself and return to love."

We not only have the healing tools given to us but we are unconditionally loved by the Divine, who understands how difficult it is to live on this dimension of limited understanding. Here we are learning to go beyond our ego, to love and spread light, albeit in the state of being perfectly imperfect!

A Message from the Lady of Light

While meditating on being human and the many states of being we experience in this realm, the beautiful presence I know as the Lady of Light gave me an empowering message.

I realised that humanity was on the verge of uncovering the Divine Feminine within us as we evolve in human consciousness. I realised that the Divine Feminine and the Divine Masculine are states of being within everyone and do not refer to gender as we understand it. We have all been in the masculine energy while we used our rational mind to make sense and measure the outer world.

The next step of the human journey is to experience the feminine energy fully, the inner mystical awareness of everything. When we do that we shall become aware that we need to integrate the head and the heart. We will probably then realise that we have always been the one light, a state of existence where the concept of forgiveness does not exist. Here are her words.

> *Since emerging from the light to enter the realms of individuality (in Divine duality) you have carried me inside you. You have made many an allegiance to honour me, Grail Seeker. You have made lifetimes of struggle and joy in my name. You have fought your brothers and sisters in my name. You have loved and lost.*
>
> *You have quested, dreamed and prophesied in search of the Holy Grail. You have encountered me in Isis, in Astarte, in Tapoat, in Our Lady of Guadalupe, the Lady in the Lake, in Mary Magdalene, as the Faerie Queen, as Pacha Mama and significantly in the Rose and the*

Cross, and in many, many more human expressions of the Divine Feminine.

You have spent many days and nights looking for me outside yourself. You are enchanted with the quest because it is in your very being. You are the genetic embodiment of light. And all the time you have been searching for your self—the one within.

You are the Quest, the Holy Grail.

You are the self-fulfilling prophecy. The time is now!

Now you, a pioneer of the emerging Nation of Magi, are standing at an evolutionary crossroads upon the journey of consciousness.

You are travelling the Divine imagination, the gift of the Mother. The I-Magi-Nation is awakening within you.

You will be shown many dreams of Man. You can stay enchanted in these dreams and diversions, but be sure that you are vigilant. These dreams of Man are addictive. They become your only reality.

You have a choice to continue travelling within the inferno, where restrictions, limitations, fighting for the cause and feeling powerless are possible.

You can stay and battle in this world where fear has become consensus reality, a world full of struggle and exhaustion. Free will operates in this realm of the great forgetting.

Or you can take the path of least resistance and surrender to the peace that passeth all understanding.

I am there. Come to me. Surrender all.

In this awareness you shall uncover and release, and in so doing your authentic self shall emerge to radiate the next world of evolutionary consciousness that awaits your embodiment.

But know that whatever road you choose I am with you always, waiting silently.

I am you and you cannot fail to remember.

I am the light of the world. I am you.

A Healing Affirmation for Grief

Every tear, every pain of loss, is a testament to our love.
Till we meet again –
I am held by my body, soul and Spirit in love.
I am never alone. I walk with angels and guides.
And this too shall pass.

"May your prayer of
listening deepen enough
to hear in the depths
the laughter of god."

—from *To Bless the Space Between Us: A Book of Blessings* by John O'Donohue

Beyond the Veil

Connecting to Signs and Messages from Beyond

Patricia

Bringing Death to Life is about embracing the Spiritual gifts that are ours for the taking on our Earthly journey—one which is only a step on a path that we can never see in full from our proximity here on Earth. It is only when we rise up from our bodies and embrace the light from which we come, and to which we return, that we can see the whole picture.

Loss—deeply painful as it is—is only ever temporary, and if we could see from a distance what our guides and angels witness, we would be reassured of this.

However, the reality is that for as long as we are alive, we reside here on Earth, and even those of us with the greatest faith in a life beyond death still succumb to the challenges and pitfalls of the events that happen to us, grief included. As we grapple with a sense of emptiness, of longing, or of sheer wonder, and perhaps even existential crisis, at what has become of a loved one who has passed over, we can lose sight of meaningful connections to our loved ones that can still be made.

When we heighten our awareness and deliberately set about connecting in to the signs and messages that are delivered from beyond, by those who remain connected to us, not alone can it help relieve the sense of grief we feel, it can also give larger meaning to our own lives, as well as helping us to feel less alone, and in the presence of a Divine plan that has our well-being at its heart.

This has certainly been my experience with my mother and father, and even my cats—the latter whose loss I felt acutely, as any animal lover will understand—and I'd like to share with you how awakening to signs and messages has been a soothing balm for me many times, and can be for you also.

One such event was during the writing of this book, when I stayed with Pam for a few days at her lovely home in Horwich. The trip was completely unplanned. I was scheduled to go to a party for my publisher's thirtieth anniversary, and had mentioned to Pam that I was dreading the palaver that goes with traipsing through Heathrow and getting the train into London. It was less than a month since I'd had major surgery and I felt very flat and tired.

Pam kindly offered to fly to Dublin and fly back to London with me. I wouldn't hear of it, but out of the blue I heard myself say, "Why don't I fly to Manchester, stay the night and we'll make an event of it?" And so it was decided: from there we'd head to London together, stay over, visit Kensington Palace to see the various exhibitions and return to Manchester.

Pam suggested I stay so that we could work on the book together, and it couldn't have happened more fortuitously. I flew to Manchester on the Saturday, a lovely flat-calm day—even the sea from above was as tranquil and glass-like as the calm before a storm sets in. On the Monday when I was originally due to fly, Hurricane Ophelia hit Ireland and ninety flights out of Dublin were cancelled. While storm-force winds battered Ireland, Pam and I glided serenely on a fast train to London, where the temperature was unseasonally balmy.

After our delightful unexpected sojourn, we came back to Horwich the following evening and made our writing plans.

I was treated like a queen, not allowed to lift a finger, and on the Thursday morning, after a mug of strong tea and a bacon butty in bed, I opened my computer and wrote the first line of my introduction: "I first became "intimate" with Death when my beloved mother passed in 2007."

Later, as we worked together in Pam's front room, I heard the words "Pick a card," as if a voice had spoken to me. Pam has several sets of cards, including Angel, Mary Magdalene and Miracle cards, with inspiring messages and profound words of wisdom. I shuffled the fifty Miracle cards and chose one, affirming a belief that underlies the first line I had written earlier.

"Intimacy."

I couldn't believe it. What were the odds of having written the line about becoming "intimate" with Death, and choosing that particular card? It affirmed my belief that we have to become intimate with Death so that it can live side by side with us and be integrated into our lives, with love, compassion and acceptance.

We knew, without the shadow of a doubt, as we sat working in beautiful harmony on that dreary wet day, that we were very much being guided by our loved ones who have passed.

Pam picked a card from the Magdalene pack and our jaws dropped. Which card, out of forty-five, had she chosen? "Intimacy."

Out of 140 cards, including the Angel series, which gave us "Celebration," our message was to share the *intimacy* of Death with you, our precious readers, as we are all on this amazing journey together.

It affirmed for us that we were doing the right thing in writing our book and gave us the courage to share personal and private details with you in an effort to spread the word that death is not the end.

We knew, without the shadow of a doubt, as we sat working in beautiful harmony on that dreary wet day, that we were very much being guided by our loved ones who have passed. We could almost feel their excitement that the knowledge was being shared and the veil that hangs between us was thinning.

I felt that I should draw a card for you, dear readers, and the one that came was "Personal Power." Reclaim your power to connect with loved ones who have gone before us. We can all do it. Stay open. Believe the connection is there. Don't try too hard. Let the signs come easily and gently, and your lives will be enriched, your sadness and grief gently assuaged: they are only a thought away.

When my mother died, Aidan assured me that she was very close and that I would receive signs from her. I hoped against hope that what he said was true and that it would happen. But I wondered if I would imagine things happened because I so badly wanted to know that she was still around.

We held her funeral on a sunny, breezy day and I looked at the prisms of light shining into the church through the stained-glass windows. As the priest said the lovely prayer of commendation—"May the angels lead you into Paradise; may the martyrs come to welcome you and take you into the holy city, the new and eternal Jerusalem. May choirs of angels welcome you and lead you to the bosom of Abraham; and where Lazarus is poor no longer may you find eternal rest"—a beam of multi-coloured light suddenly shone along the length of her coffin. A sense of great peace descended on the family, and for a moment we were comforted, knowing that she was with us.

Two weeks later, on the morning we were to bring her ashes for burial in her home place of Rosslare Harbour, I was awakened by three sharp knocks on the bedroom window. I knew it was her. I was sure I could hear her voice saying, "Get up. There's things to be done. Soon it will be over."

It was a long day, driving to Wexford, worrying about my dad and how he would bear up, worrying about my siblings and how they were coping, having to meet and greet the family and friends who waited for us at the graveyard. It was like having a second funeral, exhausting and grief-filled.

I stayed with my dad for a couple of weeks following my mother's death, and when I finally went home I lay in my bed that first night absolutely shattered, bereft, and wondering how my dad was getting on alone. I began to cry, and a certain scent enveloped me. Lily of the Valley, Nivea Creme, Max Factor face powder: all that was familiar when my mother used to kiss and hug me. She was with me again, bringing her unique motherly comfort just as she used to when she was alive. It was a balm to my weary soul.

The most direct sign she ever gave me was when I had to make a decision on which of two publishers I should sign a contract with.

I was driving up to visit my dad, as I did every day, and as I sat at a red light I was mulling over the choices. I had to decide sooner rather than later. Suddenly a little white van shot up alongside me in the inside lane. In big red font, against the white background were the letters "S&S." I was astonished and started to laugh. My mother was making it clear in no uncertain terms whom she wanted me to sign with.

Over the years since her death, there have been numerous times when I know my mother has given a sign to guide me in my life choices and my sister has shared similar experiences—where clarifying synchronicities happen just when they're most needed.

Watch for signs. Ask for them. In the simplest way, they will be given to you.

When my father passed, almost ten years after my mother, I was in no doubt that I would receive signs from him. We often discussed the ones my mother used to send. He loved hearing about them and often had them from her himself, once he had opened himself up to them. One of the best we ever had came during our first Christmas without her. We were at my sister's house for dinner, trying hard to put on the best front we could, but still devastated by our loss.

My mother had always made her own custard for the Christmas pudding, and wouldn't have any truck with ready-to-pour from a packet. My sister and I would fib and say we made our own, covertly pouring Bird's into the jug when it was our turn to host Christmas dinner.

When it was time to serve the pud, my dad said, with a twinkle in his eye, "Is that homemade custard?"

"Of course it is," my sister assured him, without batting an eyelid. At the next moment the Christmas tree shook, a bauble bounced down the branches and hopped across the floor with a great clatter. We looked at each other wordlessly, then burst out laughing. She was with us and we knew *exactly* how she felt about ready-made custard!

So, I knew that after he died my dad's signs would come and that, knowing him, they would be fairly spectacular. One of the first he gave us occurred when my brother found a reference in some papers he was going through to my grandfather's death.

My dad's father was a lighthouse keeper and had been on the Tuskar Rock lighthouse during the Second World War. A mine had drifted up against the rocks and exploded, mortally wounding my grandfather. He survived long enough to be taken ashore to hospital, but died the following day, on 3 December, the same date as my dad's death. We were amazed but not really surprised that Dad would choose to go on the same date as his own father.

Dad's signs always involve the colour green and they can be impressive. My first "colourful" post-death encounter happened when I was in Wicklow, in my mobile home a few months after he had passed. I was fast asleep and a sharp knock on the bedroom window woke me up. I looked outside. It was a beautiful clear night and the star-studded sky was magical. I wrapped a blanket around myself and went out onto the veranda. There is a thirty-two-acre field in front of my plot, and a beautiful view over to the hills, which are patchworked in vibrant greens, rich gold, and loamy, Earthy browns. I was alone. The knock I describe had a clear, sharp sound—different from someone just tapping on the window—and, strange as it may sound, my first thought on hearing it was that someone had passed over.

The signs from my parents have taken the sting out of their death. I miss them so much. I miss their hugs and conversation and the fun we had, but now I know beyond doubt that they are walking my path with me, that they are there when I need them, and we are never parted.

Then I saw it: a light was flashing against a small satellite dish nestled in the yellow gorse. Who, I thought, is out in the field at three a.m. with a torch? Yet I could see no one. The flashing continued.

Then a green light began to flicker around the edge of the satellite dish, and I watched in fascination, wondering what was unfolding.

Then it hit me. I recalled how often I'd heard Dad tell me about taking his Morse-code exams when he was studying for his tickets. Morse was used between ships during the war, when silence was a matter of life and death, because German U-boats were stalking them. I stayed watching the flashing light for another while, and felt deeply in my bones that Dad was signalling to me. That old closeness returned, and it was very comforting.

The signs I get from my dad now always contain the colour green, and often a flash of green light. His sense of humour is still as apparent as it was when he was "alive."

The signs from my parents have taken the sting out of their death. I miss them so much. I miss their hugs and conversation and the fun we had, but now I know beyond doubt that they are walking my path with me, that they are there when I need them, and we are never parted.

Trusting the "Knowing" in Your Bones

A great friend of mine, who has listened to me talk about signs and messages, told me recently about an experience she'd had. She was having a very difficult time. She'd had a heart attack, and cancer surgery the previous year, and now her daughter was ill in hospital. Both women were very stressed.

"Please, please," my friend begged her mother, who had been dead for many years, "please send me a sign that everything will be okay." She was driving in the city and began to feel disappointed that nothing was happening when she turned a corner and saw, across the street from her, a huge billboard that read, "This ends now."

A sensation of peace overcame her, and she knew this was the sign from her mother she had asked for. Later that day, her daughter rang to say she had been put on a new tablet: her pain, and the side-effects from her other medication, had lessened considerably, and she would soon be discharged. My friend said she sounded like herself again.

I was having our annual Christmas lunch with a dear friend and fellow author. It was bitterly cold, grey, and threatening snow outside, as we sat at a window table, snug and warm, in the cosy little bistro around the corner from me, tucking into a delicious meal. We hadn't seen each other for a while so we had a lot to catch up on.

I was telling her about our progress on *Bringing Death to Life*, then about the signs my dad was sending me. Also a journalist, she has always been wary of anything that can't be explained, but she has always listened to what Aidan and I have experienced with keen interest.

So, when she told me about an inexplicable event that had occurred, I was all ears. One morning, she'd had a phone call from a colleague to say that a mutual friend—we'll call her Nicole—had died. The funeral arrangements weren't yet announced.

The following day, she saw the death notice in the paper, saying that Nicole had been cremated, and a memorial service would be held at a later date.

My friend was gutted. Nicole had been a vibrant, sociable, well-known personality in media circles, with many friends. She would have loved nothing more than to have had a big funeral and a party afterwards to celebrate her life. But it was not to be.

A week later my friend was working at her desk. Suddenly Nicole's essence came to her very strongly, and an overwhelming compulsion came over her to go to Glasnevin crematorium. Why, though? She was puzzled. Her friend was already cremated. But the compulsion became more intense as she resisted this unfathomable notion.

She put on her make-up, grabbed her coat and hurried over there. The gate was closed. A man on the other side saw her peering through and explained that there were no cremations that day. He asked her whose she was looking for. She gave him Nicole's name and he told her to drive to the crematorium on the Naas road.

The same compulsion that had made her leave her desk and go to Glasnevin was now urging her to make the long drive across the city. All the while, she felt Nicole close by.

When she got to the crematorium, she parked in an almost empty car park. Yet she *knew* she had to stay. A while later a hearse arrived. The driver and an undertaker got out. She asked if they were there for a cremation. They were.

She asked if it was that of her friend. It was.

As they were speaking, two cars drove into the car park: Nicole's daughters and her sisters. They looked shocked to see my friend there. Nicole's sisters later confided that they were very upset that their sister hadn't had the funeral she deserved, but were powerless to act as their nieces had insisted on a private one.

As my friend sat at the short service she felt an enormous sense of peace envelop her, and knew her dear friend was telling her that she wanted her to be there—sure proof that her vivacious Spirit lived on.

Messages from loved ones who have passed come in many forms: a song on the radio, a sign on a bus or billboard, a scent of roses or other perfume, a line in a book that you open at random. Simply ask, then wait patiently, and you'll be pleasantly surprised. The feeling of intimacy that is created between you and your loved one—the understanding that, really, they are very close and only a thought away—helps to dissipate the cold, harsh sense of separation that loss has wrought.

As Socrates wisely said, "Death may be the greatest of all human blessings."

Aidan

What the Angels Tell Us

The angels tell us not to be afraid to ask our loved ones who have passed over to send us signs. They are still around us, so if you feel disconnected from them, or you need to know they are with you or want guidance from them, ask them to send you a sign. The more you ask, the more aware you will become of them, and the signs all around you. Give gratitude to them, and out of your doubt and fear, light and joy will return to your life.

The first time I asked my mother to send me a sign I was on my way to Wexford. It was about two months after her death and I was feeling miserable, very alone and disconnected from Spirit and my angels. So I said to her, "If you are around me, Mam, please send me a sign. Send me a car with "44" on the number plate." I selected it because of its status in sacred numerology as an angelic number.

Within a couple of seconds a car passed me on the motorway with "44" on the registration plate. Well, I thought, that's too easy, so I asked Mam again to send me a car, this time with the 44 in a certain place on the plate. For the second time a car passed with the 44 and, surprise, surprise, the number appeared as I had asked. I was amazed.

"Thank you, Mam," I said, with heartfelt gratitude. A moment later, another car passed with the 44 in the same place. As it drove by, I could hear my mother say, "There you are now, my doubting Thomas. I am with you and always will be."

Now when I am in my car, I see these numbers and know she is by my side helping and supporting me in every way.

On another occasion I had to make a decision, so I went for a drive to clear my head. As I talked to Mam, I asked her to send me a sign as to whether or not I should go ahead with my plan, make the changes and accept the work I was offered. I asked her to let a blue BMW pass me within the next few minutes if the answer was yes. I continued to drive and soon a blue BMW passed me on the road. I decided I would accept the work on offer. But, being me, I considered further and felt that sign was too easy. There were lots of BMWs on the road. I should have asked Mam for a Rolls-Royce.

Just as that thought came into my head, I rounded a corner and drove past a church. What was parked outside but a gleaming, beribboned Rolls-Royce awaiting a newly married couple. I laughed, and could imagine my lovely mam laughing as well. You didn't mess with her in life, and now I knew she was just as strong on the other side.

Never be afraid to ask for a sign from your loved ones, and make it easy for them, and for yourself: tell them the sign you want them to show you. It can be numbers, feathers, a song, a poem, a message on the side of a bus. See what resonates with and works for you. You will be very pleasantly surprised, I promise.

Patricia

I can think of no better way to kick off Mary Helen's contribution to this chapter on signs and messages from beyond than to share an email she sent to Pam, Aidan and myself following our first meeting with the publisher.

Dear Darlings,

A few weeks ago when we were sitting around the discussion table in Hachette headquarters, trying to think of a new name for our book, the tea arrived and my mug had a black bear on it. I smiled because my dad (Coach) loved black bears—they are native to our region in the Blue Ridge mountains of Virginia. I suddenly felt him close by. If you recall, Pam was sitting across the table with that "deer in the headlights" look when she, too, became aware that Dad was "in the room."

In that moment, I literally heard his booming voice say, *"Bringing Death to Life."*

Later that afternoon, I phoned Mom to tell her the good news about the book and how Dad had made an appearance. Mom then asked me if I remembered making a photo album when I was young for one of their wedding anniversaries. I had taken pictures from a worn-out album and made a fresh new honeymoon book to display their treasured memories. Mom said that the morning of our meeting she had awakened thinking about that album. She was especially thinking about Dad's favourite picture—the one where he is sharing his Coca-Cola with a black bear. She even went so far as to get out of bed to find the picture. When I told her about the bear mug and Dad's voice clearly saying, *"Bringing Death to Life,"* in my ear, she was thrilled!

She felt like Dad had made her a part of it all by planting the image of the picture in her head. She was delighted to receive a phone call to say that he had shown up, heralded by the black bear mug . . . Amazing! When I phoned her from Ireland at 2.30 p.m., it was 9.30 a.m., for her, and she had just found the picture when the phone rang.

This pic arrived in the post today and Mom wanted you all to see it. If things continue with the same kind of magic we've started with, I think we're looking at a book that will bring true peace and comfort to many.

With big black bear hugs,

MH

So, thank you, Mr Hensley, for giving us this beautiful title and perfectly illustrating the whole premise of this book, that death is not the end, life goes on, and great help comes to us from those who have passed on.

Awakening to signs and messages is not complicated, it is a matter of opening up our awareness and belief that it is possible. It is a matter of asking your higher power.

Mary Helen

From the time of my earliest memory, I have had an intimate connection with the world of Spirit, receiving signs and messages throughout my life. Although I consider this connection a great gift, it has not always been an easy one.

But it gives me immense joy to be able to connect people in my work with those who they have lost, often detailing private information that is enormously comforting to them at their time of grief. When my clients awaken to the idea that they can be connected autonomously with a lost loved one—that they do not need me to mediate—they find it life-changing, and often report over time remarkable incidents where they felt the intervention of their loved one at times of need, or special family times where they are most missed. Awakening to signs and messages is not complicated, it is a matter of opening up our awareness and belief that it is possible. It is a matter of asking your higher power.

Pennies from Heaven

Tricia and I love to have a chance to be together, sitting in her house in our jammies, fire ablaze, tucking into some magnificent, homemade dish that my children would affectionately refer to as "real food" (I'm not noted for my culinary skills). We are completely at ease in each other's company: no make-up, no formalities, no fuss. We laugh until we actually cry, we share our trials and tribulations, we plot and plan adventures, we talk about upcoming storylines for books, and we eat all of the "guilty pleasures" we want, because in the midst of true friendship, calories are a figment of the imagination. Between us, we have plenty of imagination to spare.

Although I never knew Tricia's mother, I know that her relationship with her was like mine today with my own mom. They took adventures together, talked daily and really were the best of pals. She grieved her passing deeply, and missed her physical presence terribly, despite her knowledge that her mother was safe in the hands of the Divine.

From the time I first met Tricia, her mom became a regular and welcome part of our conversations. Tricia would always remind me to relish every precious moment with my own mother. For me, that's a piece of cake.

My mother, Sweet Helen, or Mama Helen, as Tricia calls her, was delighted to meet my bestie in the flesh two years ago. They are constantly exchanging letters, emails and gifts. Tricia and I often video-chat with Mama Helen when we're having one of our infamous sleepovers. In short, they have adopted one another. When Mom first set foot in Tricia's house, it was like a homecoming: the two rejoiced in each other's company.

I have never known someone with such genuine veneration for the Mother energy as Tricia. She is forever making reference to the Blessed Mothers, to Mary, to Magdalene, Bridget, the wise woman, tradition, and the ancestry of women who have shaped the Divine Feminine on this planet.

Mom wasn't long through the door when she was shown one of my favourite photographs of Tricia and her own mother, taken soon after Tricia's first book was published. Mom remarked on how beautiful her mother was, as if she were right there in the room with us. Tricia and I smiled: "Sweet Helen" really is so sweet.

Later that evening, when talk turned to how Tricia was celebrating the twenty-fifth anniversary of the release of her first novel *City Girl*, a silver coin—an old Irish punt to be exact—fell out of nowhere at our feet. It landed just after Tricia had given Mom a hug and expressed how much she missed her own mother's hugs. That silver coin, out of circulation since 2002, had materialised as if from thin air and hit the floor as we were speaking about the book's silver anniversary. We erupted into laughter, pure joy and certain celebration that Tricia's beloved mother was acknowledging her daughter's literary achievements.

One of my greatest pleasures as a metaphysician is when other people witness, at first hand, the Divine at work in their lives. It's lovely to read about it or to hear someone else share, but to be there when a person sees it with their own two eyes is priceless.

So often I have received messages from people all around the world telling me they have heard from a loved one in the form of coins appearing out of nowhere. I've often wondered, why coins? Is it easier for a Spirit, an energetic being, to manipulate the physical mass of a small coin? Is the coin itself significant in some way? Who knows? But it is a repeated theme and I am quite sure that our loved ones are never far away—if they want you to know that they are there, they will even drop pennies from Heaven to let you know they love you.

The afternoon I finished writing this story, I picked my girls up from school as usual. After talking to another mom in the parking lot, I opened my car door and gasped. There, perfectly placed in the centre of my seat, was a brand new shiny penny gleaming up at me. It definitely hadn't been there before and I wasn't wearing anything with pockets from which it could have fallen.

My daughter Jemma, knowing nothing of what I had been writing about earlier, turned to me and, in a very matter-of-fact tone, informed me that the penny was from Tricia's father.

"How do you know that?" I asked. My extremely sensitive and highly attuned teenager shot me the exact same look I give her when she asks me how I know things. "*Touché*, little girl." I could do nothing but laugh. I took a photo of the penny and sent it to Tricia, knowing she would be delighted by the synchronicity at play.

A Voice in My Ear

At the end of May 2005, I decided to take a break from my extremely hectic life as a full-time chiropractor and single mom of two girls, ages one and three. The last few years had been difficult: I needed some breathing space and a long-overdue visit with my mom and dad. My father had lost a very dear friend to cancer the day before I arrived in Virginia from Ireland. There's nothing like the suffering of another to put your own sorrows into perspective.

The one request this man had made was that Dad assist him in writing his own eulogy, then deliver their combined sentiments at his funeral. Dad had participated in countless funeral services; his presence and conviction in his faith had seen many families through difficult times over the years.

This time, though, was different. Due to a sudden turn in his lifelong friend's situation, Dad had been unable to sit with Turner and make good on his request to co-author the final musings of his life. Dad was really struggling, as the onus was now on him to capture the words Turner would have used of his time on Earth.

The day before the funeral, I walked into the kitchen to find Dad sitting in his seat at the head of the table, staring at the same page of the yellow legal pad he had been staring at when I had gone to bed the night before. It wasn't that he didn't know what to say: it was that his friend had so much wanted to be a part of this process and hadn't lived long enough to do it. Stock standard sentiment was simply not an option, and Dad was humbly attempting to find just the right words to pay tribute to Turner's life.

I sat down at the other end of the table with a bowl of oatmeal. Before I got the first spoonful into my mouth I heard *a voice*. I looked to my right, where Mom was pottering around the kitchen listening to the radio. Dad was in the same position, pen in hand, across the table. I had just taken a bite of my breakfast when I heard it again.

"Remind him of when I used to swap him milkshakes for Coca-Cola at the drug-store lunch counter."

I put my spoon down and looked at my mother, who was now aware that something strange was going on.

"What is it?" she whispered, from across the room.

I shrugged my shoulders, looking back at Dad, who was still staring at his sparse notes. I had gone back to my breakfast when I heard the same voice, now laughing.

"Be sure to say the milkshakes were strawberry. Dick loved his strawberry shakes!"

I got up and walked into the living room. Mom followed me, knowing from my face that something was up.

"Mom, I think Mr Weaver is talking to me!"

"Really? What did he say?" She was excited and a little freaked out.

I had just relayed the first two messages when suddenly the voice started again, this time going into a full history of when Turner Weaver and Dad had played on the old gravel field at Brown Street as kids. He went on to discuss their circle of friends in detail, even calling one by a nickname that only a member of that tight-knit group could have known.

By this time, Mom had gone into the kitchen and told Dad what was happening, as the messages continued to flow. Turner was fulfilling his wish to participate in the writing of his eulogy with my dad. A bit stunned but unable to deny the accuracy of the memories, Dad was given the details that would complete his friend's final request. Turner had shed his broken body and spoken from Spirit.

He even asked that Dad use a specific passage from a certain prayer book entitled *It's Never Too Late to Start Over*. I enjoyed hearing those first-hand accounts of my father's youth, however unconventional the means. As Turner Weaver and my father reminisced together one last time, we all got a bit emotional when Turner exclaimed, "Oh, boy, oh, boy, Dick! Just wait till you see it here!"

The following day, I stood in the back corner of a packed church and watched as people nodded, shed a few tears but mostly smiled and laughed as they, too, reminisced with Turner while Dad delivered the most beautiful and uplifting eulogy. Everyone left feeling they had celebrated the man's life.

After the service, a very dear family friend, an elderly but extremely lively character, joked with Dad in private, upon hearing about earlier events. He elbowed Dad, chuckled and said, "When I die, Dick, I'm going to send you a message." With that, Jack whispered something into Dad's ear. Only he would know the quirky line his old pal had pledged to deliver from beyond the grave.

There was no better man to do it. I absolutely loved him. His voice had reminded me of a cartoon character I'd liked when I was a child and his laugh was incredibly distinctive. Jack had a tremendous sense of humour and, in his late eighties, had been known to drive around town in a hearse just for a laugh!

When Jack passed away, less than a year after Turner, I was sitting in bed at my home in Ireland when I heard an unmistakable voice. I immediately rang home to Virginia and told my folks that I had just heard the strangest message from our departed friend, Jack.

"Tell Dick I'm playing Cowboys and Indians!"

The phone was dead silent at the other end.

It seemed as if an eternity had passed when Dad quietly replied, "That's *exactly* what Jack told me he'd say to me, the day of Turner Weaver's funeral."

Prayer To Help Open Up to Connections and Messages from Beyond

Higher Power
I trust in you and ask that you connect me
through signs and messages with [insert name/s].
I open myself up fully to receiving
these signs, trusting that my higher self is at all
times connected and can transmit information
from beyond the veil, through
your loving power, whenever I call upon it.

"I will not leave you as orphans, I will come to you."

—Jesus in John 14:18

The Death of Those Who Gave Us Life

Reflections on Loss of a Parent

Patricia

Most of us will experience the death of a parent. If it happens at the end of a long life, it comes with a sense of the natural. Yet, as those who have experienced the loss of a parent know, that does not make it easier or less painful. And it brings up very different emotions for different people, as the following testimonies show.

But what combines them is that, for each person, the loss of a parent has been life-changing. Although no soul is an orphan, losing a parent can make us feel that we are.

I was privileged to be with my parents at the moment of their passing. Pam wasn't with her mother, and Mary Helen was in Ireland when her dad crossed in America. And, for each of us, that was how it was meant to unfold.

How often have we heard of bedside vigils lasting for hours, sometimes days, until the family are sent off for a cuppa, or are told the loved one is in no danger so they should go home and rest? Then, unfairly, it seems, the dying person embarks on their journey of transition alone. One of the subjects we explore in the following pages is why that might be.

One of the saddest stories I ever heard was told to me by an elderly woman. In the final stages of a terminal illness, her son, who was in his thirties, came back to his homeplace to die. She had tended him lovingly during those last days, but when death came, her son expressed his wish to die alone in his room. Distraught, trying to hide her anguish, and her tears, she left him to himself.

"How were you able to do it?" I asked sympathetically.

"I understood death," she answered. "I knew he could not go if I was there." She was a beautiful countrywoman, stoic and wise, and her great unconditional love for her son gave her the strength to make an almost unendurable sacrifice for him, enabling him to make his transition beyond the veil.

Not every relationship has such a loving ending, as Aidan explains so movingly and honestly, and that's all right too. It's part of the great tapestry of our soul plan. What's important is how we deal with this most difficult of events.

Regardless of the circumstances, it is hard to move on after the loss of a family member or loved one. But this is part of the challenge, and as we become more intimate with death, our knowledge makes it easier to come to terms with our loss and, ultimately, face our own passing.

Here we share our personal stories of the loss of a parent.

My Mother's Passing

"Are you afraid?" I asked my mother.

"No," she said calmly. "Are you?"

"No," I answered resolutely, although inwardly I was quaking. I had never seen anyone die, and I was shaken to my core, in deep shock that my beloved mother was coming to the end of her Earthly existence. I couldn't begin to imagine life without her.

And then I heard myself say—I don't know where it came from: "You know I'm here to help you on your journey."

Mammy smiled and we squeezed hands. "You know what you have to do," she said.

"Don't worry, I know. We'll all do what needs to be done, and we'll look after Dad," I assured her.

"I have no worries," she said.

We were in a small curtained-off cubicle in the high-dependency unit of a large hospital. The compassion and kindness of the nurses and doctors gave us a little comfort. Otherwise machines bleeped incessantly. The lights were harsh. The ward was noisy, with trolleys clattering, hoovers, conversations, as life outside our small, sterile domain carried on as normal.

It shouldn't be like this, I thought miserably. But these were our circumstances as my mother prepared to make her transition from this world to the next.

Later, during that long night, as our family sat in vigil around her bed, I would ask the nurse if we could at least light a candle. "I'm sorry," she said gently. "It would be too dangerous with the oxygen."

I remember thinking of all the people I knew who had lost a parent or loved one, and while I had the utmost sympathy for them, and thought I understood their grief, I really had no conception of the reality. *So this is what it's like,* I thought, as I joined the club of which no one wishes to become a member.

But, despite my grief and trauma, what resonated very strongly with me, as the night passed and dawn broke, was how privileged I was to be with my mother as she, with immense grace and dignity, ended that chapter in her book of eternal existence and began the next.

At that powerful moment of death, passing, transitioning—so many ways of describing it—I sensed her being released from her ailing body, and her Spirit expanding as she was freed from its confines. At that awe-inspiring instant, I was absolutely convinced there was so much more to my mother than I had known of her. That her "energy," her "being," was her *true* self and that while her body was no longer alive, *she* very much was.

It was a comfort of sorts, which would grow stronger over the years. But at that moment, the shock, indescribable sadness, and understanding that I would never see her again, never be hugged and kissed by her, never talk to her or take her on one of our girls' jaunts in *this* life left me utterly bereft.

In that very moment life changed to "before" and "after," and as my precious mother went on her new journey, my family and I set off on a long, hard road and a new journey of our own.

Aidan

My Father's Passing

"The most painful goodbyes are the ones that are never said and never explained." —Balil Nasir Khan

The knock came on the door late that Friday evening. It was my brother with bad news. The hospital had called, and my father was about to pass over. He was not expected to last the night. We were to come as soon as possible.

The city was cold, dark and empty as we drove to the hospital, wondering what awaited us. The night porter let us in. When we got to my dad's ward the curtains were pulled around his bed and I could hear his laboured breathing, even from the doorway.

We sat around his bed, feeling helpless. What could we do? My mother told us to pray and ask God to take him. He had suffered enough. His quality of life had gone. He wanted to go. She had spoken with him earlier that day, and he had told her he wanted to die. He had suffered for more than a year, had both his legs amputated, had contracted TB and, that morning, he'd been given the news that he had cancer of the tongue. Could things get any worse?

We'd had a few of these scenarios over the past months, getting the call from the hospital, rushing in, sitting by his bed, but he'd always pulled through within a matter of hours. This time, though, something was different. The stillness and the quiet were so beautiful, and a soft mist seemed to cover us in the dimly lit ward.

Yet, as I looked at my father struggling to breathe, and tried to pray for him, I felt nothing. Who was the man in the bed I was sitting beside? He was my father in name, but he'd never felt like a dad. During the year of his illness, I'd got to know him a little better, but not to love him or know him in the way I wanted to. He was as cold in his illness as he was in his health. Alone. Just on the edge. Never giving anything away.

I so desperately wanted him to say, "I love you, son, and I'm sorry I wasn't there for you." But, on the other hand, even though I knew he was dying, I couldn't tell him I loved him either. The wall that had always been between us was still there, and I believed then that it would never come down. It was all I could think of that night as I sat and watched and hoped that God in His mercy and love would take him.

The nurse came in to check him over the next couple of hours and all she could say was "No change. He is still very low." Later she offered us tea and told us to go to the visitors' room. The rest of the family left, and I stayed with Mam. She was upset, and for the first time I could remember, she took my father's hand and held it. She prayed, then told him to let go and be at peace. I took his other hand, and Mam and I just looked at each other. The silence was beautiful and his breathing became easier.

"I think he's going," Mam said. With that, he opened his eyes and looked at her, then me. His eyes were glassy, and in one swift motion he pulled his hand away from mine.

My heart sank. There was no softening, even in his hour of death. Why did he hate me so much? I was gutted.

I left the ward and went to tell the family he was awake. I stayed in the visitors' room and had a cup of tea while they returned to his bedside.

I waited for about half an hour and saw the doctor go to my father, then to the family. Then I saw them all leave the ward. Mam came in and told me my father had come round, once more, and was out of danger. We were advised to go home and rest.

I left the hospital knowing I wouldn't see him again. I'd really tried, but that was it for me. It seemed clear now that he didn't want or need me around.

"Felix the Cat," I remember saying to my sister on the way home. "That's what we should call him." It seemed that my dad also had nine lives.

Over the next couple of days, Dad seemed to improve: he started to eat and drink a little again. The family went in turn to visit him, but I didn't.

On the following Monday, I visited Mam on my lunch break and she phoned the hospital to see how he was. They told her he was doing very well: he had just eaten his lunch and was talking. They told her to take her time coming in as he was fine. I went back to work, and at two thirty my sister-in-law phoned me, saying the hospital couldn't get in contact with my mother to tell her that my father had passed away in his sleep at about two o'clock.

I couldn't believe it. My mind went blank. He died as he'd lived, alone and with no family around him. I went to see him in the hospital, a couple of hours after his passing. He looked at peace, and about twenty years younger. All the pain had left him and I could feel a presence around him. He's safely home, I thought.

The words "my dad died" did not come naturally to me. I had practised them during his illness, in an attempt to put into them some kind of heartfelt thought or emotion that, in truth, I couldn't summon. "My dad died." Those words described everything and nothing. They meant nothing to me, maybe because he had always been dead to me in some way.

The days leading up to his funeral were strange. I still felt nothing. I couldn't cry and didn't feel bad about it. I made the arrangements for his funeral with Mam and, if I'm honest, I was filled with relief, a sense of freedom.

At the funeral when the priest spoke of my father, and people sympathised with me, I didn't much recognise the man they were talking about. The lovely kind gentleman, who was such a pleasure to talk to, was not the man I knew or had ever seen. When I think of him, an old saying always comes to mind: "Any man can be a father, but not every man can be a dad." I had never experienced the father—son bond of love, so how could I grieve or even react to his death?

They say grief comes in different ways and at different times. It is hard dealing with the loss of a parent and perhaps harder still when you feel nothing for them. You feel guilty because you're supposed to love—or at least like—your parents and mourn their passing. Little did I know what lay ahead for me in the years to come, and how hard I would struggle to find the dad I never knew in life. But I did find him and I forgave him, and even loved him in death, in a way I never could in life. He taught me many lessons, and offered me one great gift: that of understanding, forgiveness, and that I should never judge because we all have our own path to follow and our own choices to make.

Mary Helen

Dad's passing

My father was eighty-five years old when he died, after a long and good life, the last years of which were more difficult, as he battled the dual challenges of Alzheimer's and congestive heart failure.

Before the last days of his life, it would have been hard for me to imagine not being present at his death. After all, I've been present at many deaths in my lifetime, and it is something that I consider myself "good" at, if such a term can apply! As a metaphysician, I am at one with the process of death, intimately connected to its nuance and indeed beauty—that which comes from witnessing shifting luminosity in all its glorious manifestations.

However, in the case of my father, being present at the time of death was not to be, and my own journey in the lead-up to it revealed to me the reasons why, for Dad, it was a private affair that needed to take place away from those he loved most in this world.

As his last days drew in, it was rare for him to snap back to reality but I recall one such occasion. Mumbling and fidgety, Dad was so agitated that he couldn't get his words out.

He had been like that for a few months. He would stand in front of the mirror, staring at the body that had once been that of a world champion weight-lifter, now withered and frail ... and he would weep.

One night I wondered if Dad was even aware that I was there. I stood in front of him, looked him in the eyes and said, "Dad! Just look at me. Look into my eyes. Do you know who I am?"

He grabbed me tightly by the forearms and said, "You are Mary Helen Hensley, born on the twenty-third of February 1969 and you have managed to single-handedly and categorically reject every adult male relationship in your life."

While some might have taken offence, I burst into laughter at this brief, yet quite accurate description, and shouted, "Yes! That's right, Dad! It's me!" I remember going home in the wee hours of the morning. When I arrived, Auntie Joyce, my mother's sister and fellow insomniac, was sitting up reading a book. I told her what had happened and it gave us the opportunity to laugh until we cried at the morbidly comical duality of life.

Dad had been transferred from rehab to a nursing home. I stayed in town long enough to get him settled in, then headed back to my eagerly awaiting children in Ireland.

Although I implicitly trusted my Source, regarding Dad's final departure, I clocked up a serious amount of frequent-flyer miles between November 2011 and August 2012 to check in with Mom and sit with Dad.

As a child I had regularly and accurately dreamed about the deaths of friends and loved ones, so when I reached my early teens, I had asked my grandfather in Spirit to show me when my parents were going to die. If I was going to walk through my life with the "gift of foresight," I thought it only fair that I didn't have to live in dread of getting in a prophetic dream in my sleep about the deaths of the two people I loved most. He obliged. Many people think that this would be a terrible bit of information to carry around, but if you could put yourself in my shoes, you might see that it took a tremendous pressure off my young mind, in light of the never-ending stream of visions and dreams. In short, it has worked well for me.

When my daughters, Jemma and Jada, finished school at the end of June, we packed our bags and headed from Ireland to Virginia for the summer. I spent many late nights with Dad, watching his favourite movie, *The Quiet Man*, over and over again. He had full-time sitters in his room, as he was now a danger to himself if left alone. We had initially decorated his space, trying to give it a more home-like feel, but the photographs of his children and grandchildren upset him and had to be removed. Next to the small hospital bed, there was a simple wooden nightstand with a lamp and a single framed picture of my mother in her early twenties, her auburn hair flowing over her shoulders. Mom's college photo and his own tattered blue prayer book were the only items he allowed.

On 21 August, I climbed into bed in my old room at my parent's house. Although it had changed over the years, there were still a few of my childhood belongings: trophies for acting and sportsmanship, dolls from Scotland and my favourite Nancy Drew books on a shelf. I was weary. As someone gifted with the ability to see the auric field around a person, I had witnessed the energy in Dad's begin to change weeks earlier, from the pulsating glow of a once-vibrant human being to sparks and flashes, the pre-death fireworks I had seen so many times before.

I drifted off to sleep—only to be awakened at about three-thirty by my own screams. When my mother came in from her bedroom next door and turned on the light, I was sitting up in bed, breathless, in a cold sweat. "Are you okay?" she asked. "What is it? What happened?"

I couldn't answer. I got out of bed and walked past her to the bathroom to splash cold water on my face. She was waiting when I returned to bed. "I can't talk about it right now, Mom." Tears were streaming down my cheeks. "I'll tell you in the morning."

Instinctively knowing she shouldn't pry, Mom went back to bed.

Under the covers, I tossed and turned until, for the second time that night, I drifted into a troubled sleep. Within minutes, I sat up, panting and perspiring, this time catching myself before I screamed aloud. It was a vision.

I could see a tattered tartan, wrapped around dirty, yet feminine legs, animal-skin shoes bound with leather straps and a pair of slender yet strong hands . . . my hands. On the ground before me was a giant of a man, no less than six and a half feet, with jet-black hair, laced with straw and muck. His face was filthy, his yellowed teeth clenched as he writhed in agony. His chest was bare, bar the markings of ancient symbols that had been painted or dyed across his upper torso. On one of his legs, just below the knee, there was a gaping wound, festering and septic, the obvious source of his pain and imminent death. I heard the woman pleading with the warrior, telling him to rest, to go. She begged him to allow himself to go into the light. I could feel her pounding heart breaking as she pleaded with the man to let go of life, end his suffering and return home. At that moment, he rolled on to his side, sweat and filth matting his once impressive mane of hair. He lifted a trembling arm in her direction and gave one final command in his native tongue: "Leave me, woman. This is my death, alone." I realised, in that instant, that I was looking into the eyes of the soul who had become my father in this life.

The following morning, as my mother was getting dressed to go to the nursing home, I told her about the vision. She shook her head in disbelief as I recounted every detail of this former incarnation of my father. We were stunned, and agreed to meet later that day at the nursing home after I had run a few errands and taken the girls to the pool.

Dad's love for Scotland and the ancient Celts had come from his pride in his heritage as a descendant of Rob Roy MacGregor, Scotland's answer to Robin Hood. Although folklore had greatly added to his fame over the years, Rob Roy had been a colourful character in eighteenth-century Scottish history. "Robert the Red" was not only known by his trademark mane of red hair, but also for the distinctive birthmark under his knee, referred to as the "black knee." Dad had always been very proud of his own birthmark, under his knee, reputed to be found on any number of the male descendants of Rob Roy. I had even photographed it: Mom and I thought it would be an interesting keepsake for posterity. And now it was clear to me, from my vision of my dad as the raven-haired dying warrior, that Rob Roy was his descendant and that in this life, Dad had incarnated back in that bloodline.

That afternoon, I opened the door to Dad's room. My mother stopped me. "You're not going to believe this!" she whispered. She giggled nervously. That was always my opening line to her. She told me to pull the blanket off my father's legs. Puzzled, I walked over to the bed where Dad was in a restless sleep. "Go ahead," she urged.

When I pulled the blanket down I nearly got weak. The dark brown birthmark and distinctive black mole that, for eighty-five years, had held a place of honour on Dad's leg were gone. I did a double-take, looked at Mom and back again at his leg to make sure my eyes weren't deceiving me. *Gone.* She motioned for me to come back to the door. "Your dream last night, the vision, whatever it was . . . It's you holding him back. You've got to get out of here!" I agreed. It was as if the communication had come from the earliest ancestors of that bloodline.

My presence was stopping Dad making his transition. I had been in that situation so many times with members of a family holding vigil by the bedside of a loved one, prepared to die, but not letting go. And so many times I had encouraged them to give space to the individual to cross on their own, if they wished, in the peace of their own thoughts. Not every dying soul wants to be surrounded by the good intentions of those grieving their loss. It seems I had carelessly ignored my own advice.

I spent my last moments with Dad, thanking him and whispering vivid details of what awaited him on the other side of death, just as I had each day for the last six weeks. I kissed his forehead, his third eye, one last time, went home and changed our plane tickets for departure to Ireland the following day.

We arrived in an uncharacteristically sunny Ireland on the morning of 23 August. I left the girls with some good friends, repacked my bag and waited for the phone call. The following morning, 24 August 2012, Mom phoned to say that Dad had passed peacefully before dawn. I had been sitting on the stone wall outside my cottage, thousands of miles away, watching the sun dance across the rolling green fields when I had felt him go.

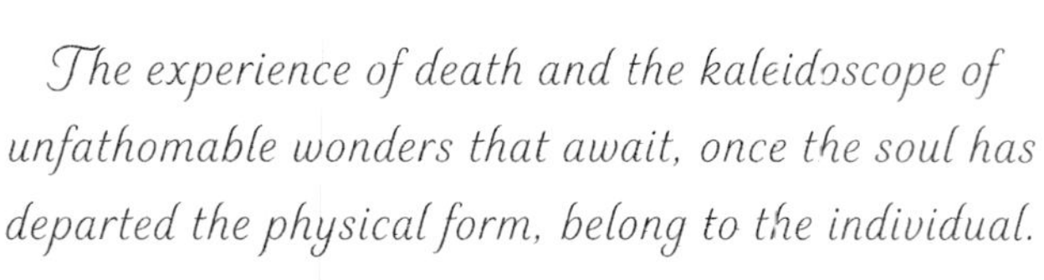

The experience of death and the kaleidoscope of unfathomable wonders that await, once the soul has departed the physical form, belong to the individual.

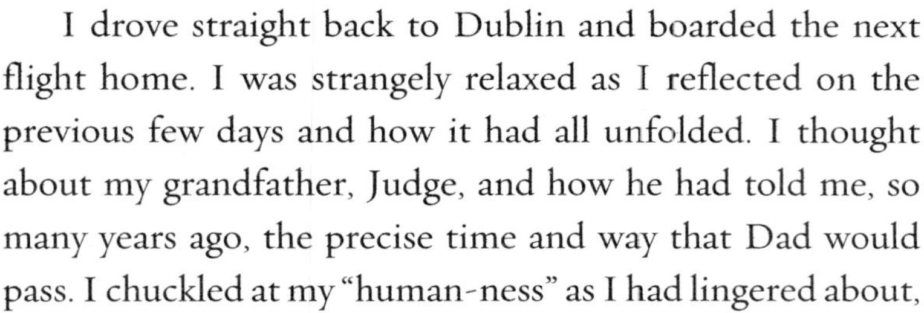

I drove straight back to Dublin and boarded the next flight home. I was strangely relaxed as I reflected on the previous few days and how it had all unfolded. I thought about my grandfather, Judge, and how he had told me, so many years ago, the precise time and way that Dad would pass. I chuckled at my "human-ness" as I had lingered about, hoping to outwit Destiny's plan, so that I could be present when the soft glow of death lifted Dad from his sleep. That had been left for a complete stranger. One of the sitters had been transformed for having witnessed the angelic presence and beautiful glow that emanated from Dad's face as his Spirit left his body.

For hours, I relaxed, legs outstretched: I had a bulkhead seat with only empty space in front of me. A movie was on the screen and I could hear the occasional laughter of those watching, but mostly there was just the hum of the engines, lulling me into a meditative state.

I thought about my decision to leave the children behind, my desire to give myself the time and space to be a daughter burying her father, rather than a mother tending her children. They had done a better job than me in making Dad's death about him, and now they were giving me the opportunity to acknowledge my own grief.

Although I had secretly wanted to bypass the plan and stay by his side, I understood that this would have made it all about me. The experience of death and the kaleidoscope of unfathomable wonders that await, belong to the individual. It may have taken me a while to practise what I preach, but in the end, I got it.

Pamela

My Mother's Passing

Like Mary Helen, I was not present at the time of my mother's death, but it was very different in that Mum's was a sudden one. And as I discovered, there is no preparation for the shock of a loved one's sudden death. There is no preparation for the utter disbelief and devastation. One moment life is content, full of blessings, and the next it is filled with excruciating pain and loss.

The day I lost my mum, the sky was blue and expansive, one of those brilliantly clear days that only an autumn sun can create. How could it be such a beautiful, life-enhancing day when my lovely mum had just left this world?

I was lost. In the hospital I said goodbye to her, but the real her had gone. Her body without her was just an empty vessel where once there had been a vibrant woman full of love, laughter, tears, stories and zest for life.

With her gift of second sight, she had shared with me so much news of the spirit world, whence we came, and to which we shall return, telling me of the many wonderful things we have to look forward to when we make the transition.

I knew she was more alive now, experiencing a higher, brighter and lighter life, free from limitations, in the Summerland, no doubt having being met by her deceased father and her baby boy, stillborn, my brother Christopher, grown-up now, in Spirit. He had been by her side since his death thirty years before. What a joyful reunion they would be having. But that knowledge did not prevent our family suffering terrible grief. The grief that rises up for months and years, unexpectedly, out of the blue, often about the little things you didn't do or say in the days before the death.

Although we had shared a great love and many wonderful times, I could focus only on the things, often inconsequential to anyone else, that I perceived had hurt her. For a long time I was full of remorse that I hadn't taken up Mum's invitation to pop in for a cuppa when I'd dropped her off after a healing service the night before she died. If only I had known it was the last time I would see her alive.

I knew in my heart that my mum understood if ever I had hurt her, or when I projected my bad moods on to her. I knew that love overrides all the misunderstandings of life, but for a long time I couldn't see beyond my grief.

With her gift of second sight, she had shared with me so much news of the spirit world, whence we came, and to which we shall return, telling me of the many wonderful things we have to look forward to when we make the transition.

But life goes on: the body keeps breathing and time heals. Family and friends are a great blessing in this time of raw vulnerability, which eventually subsides to make way for happy memories and the legacy of your loved one's life to emerge.

As the saying goes, "This, too, shall pass." And it is true.

Every day I have greeted and thanked my mum, knowing she watches over my family and me. The physical and mental pain have long gone to be replaced by enthusiasm and gratitude for my own life, filled with so much love from and for my family. Now twenty-two years on, I can talk with humour about my mum's passing, a day filled with simple delights and symbols, of a life well lived to the full, right to the very end. Her life was always in service to others. She had the capacity to see the light in everyone, to cherish and encourage them. Retired from a nursing career, she gave herself totally to her love of Spirit, sharing the knowledge of the wonderful afterlife, open to every soul. She became the president of the local Spiritualist church and dedicated her life entirely to sharing the news that we survive death, that we are guided here on Earth and are never alone.

Every Wednesday she made time for a few hours of pleasure just for herself. She loved those Wednesdays, enjoying what she called her guilty secrets. Coming out of her flat that day, she greeted her friend, Little Alice (there was also a Big Alice), with a smile of expectation for their day out.

Always taking a pride in her appearance, that day was no exception, but Little Alice said later there was something different about Mum, as if she was shining. In her high heels, her make-up understated and perfect, she wore her new winter coat of cream mohair from the high-end charity shop (Mum always loved a bargain). She looked radiant.

Catching the bus into town, they alighted at the bakery where they bought two beef and onion barms, still Mum's favourite, despite the doctor's advice to cut them out! But, after all, it *was* Wednesday—a treat day! A hop and a skip, and they were at their destination. Mecca Bingo, the place Mum kept secret because she didn't feel it was fitting for the president of the church to frequent it. A quick look over her shoulder and she was in.

Having paid their entrance fee, they made their way to their regular seats, pleased to see that no newcomers had taken them. The excitement was building as they placed their six-page booklets on the table, tested their marker pens and put their cleaned glasses on.

Tom, the caller, arrived, with a jovial "Good afternoon, ladies and gentlemen." Then, after "Eyes down. Your first number is . . ." they were off.

Towards the end of the session, according to Little Alice, Mum shouted, "Here!"—"House" was out of fashion—winning forty pounds for a full house Always sharing their winnings, they were delighted to be taking home a profit.

Eventually, after a good natter and a nice win, they ended the session, saying, "See you next week." Everyone else made their way home but Mum asked Alice to wait: she had indigestion. They sat for a while but when they tried to leave they found the hall door locked. They spotted the emergency exit and Alice attempted but failed to open it. According to Alice, Mum insisted on trying and, laughing, gave it a good hard push. The door opened—and Mum stepped forward into the light. She died on the spot.

That evening, Mum should have been chairing a special service at church, but instead an announcement was made that their wonderful president had died suddenly at bingo! Her secret was out for all to hear, announced to a packed congregation. Of course no one judged her but she was greatly missed and will never be forgotten.

I can see Mum laughing now at the way she made her grand exit from this world and her dramatic entrance to the next. Her life and death, open as a book, and revealed in all her glory.

I wonder if she still has Wednesdays off with Little Alice? I must ask her.

Prayer for Loss of a Parent

Higher power
As I am your child, hold me in your arms as I grieve the loss of my parent [insert name]. Connect me to their loving energy so that I may know them to be close, even though they are out of sight.

Connect me to all that they have given me so that I may honour them as I live, sharing those gifts each day. For any anger I harbour, heal me so that I am free from grievance, in the understanding that [insert name] has now gone to the Source where all things are healed and where there is no division.

In your name I ask that the burden be lifted from my heavy heart, and that I always know the light of love, even in my grief.

"We remember their love when they can no longer remember."

—Anon

A Living Death

Reflections on Alzheimer's and Dementia

Pamela

There are many ways of dying, and I would like to include here something I was given by Spirit on the illness that is often known as "a living death." Mary Helen has described for us the incredible journey, undertaken by her precious dad and family, as he succumbed to Alzheimer's disease.

Alzheimer's and dementia are physical conditions of the brain, not of the spirit or soul.

The person afflicted may reveal many physical reactions to brain disease, such as losing social skills, independence and the ability to self-care. If we believe, as I do, that all humanity is connected in a collective consciousness, then it is possible that diseased thinking in the world may also create pollution in our individual minds too.

It was imparted to me, as I channelled this message from Spirit, that the person with the disease may have taken it on to heal and eradicate it for our future selves.

The carers and loved ones are also deeply involved in this healing. Though disease may feel like a cruel punishment, it is quite the opposite. We are now beginning to see our huge capacity and power to destroy and to heal.

Everyone born here since time began has had a mission to bring a little more light to each and every incarnation. The light is in ascendance, shining so brightly that we are now revealing the shadows more clearly.

Thought is a living thing, as real as the air we breathe. Every situation that disturbs the equilibrium of mind and body manifests in disease, arising to be acknowledged and to be healed. Every situation comes to us as an opportunity to enlighten our path of awakening.

As the disease progresses we may see agitation and physical disorientation, as the person we have known disappears before our eyes. They are losing identification of the self that has experienced life on Earth. These things disturb us deeply, and it is sad and painful to watch as we too lose the connection, and a loved one, who can no longer remember or acknowledge. The Earthly self, which identifies with personality, beliefs and experiencing, on this lower vibration, is merely a dim reflection of the true higher self that emerges on the death of the physical being.

Dementia brings almost unbearable mourning before a loved one dies. We judge mostly from our limited perception, living here in this material realm, but we cannot know what the person who has lost identification with the physical senses is experiencing. For us it may be a horror story, but for them it may be a service of light, beyond belief.

Attaining this higher frequency of light, whilst still living and breathing on this lower frequency, may transform human consciousness as we presently know it. As we come to understand ourselves as instruments of light and not just human beings, we may get a glimpse of the human journey as it evolves in consciousness beyond the material realm.

As the person nears the end of their journey with dementia, relinquishing their identity with the brain-led awareness of reality, they may become a silent channel for higher soul awareness. Devoid of "ordinary" perceptions, we may judge them as an empty vessel, but in this state of no thought and no thing, it becomes possible to radiate only pure love, the highest possible manifestation of light on Earth. In so doing, it transmutes and enlightens humanity on Earth, as we know it.

Thanks to these wonderful souls, we shall be enlightened and, as individuals and as a collective, shall come together in healing ourselves, and the planet, of our former ignorance, which has caused dis-ease on many levels.

It may be only when we ourselves die, and we meet again with our kin, who have taken on this light service, that we will realise that love, the highest manifestation of light, can never be destroyed. We shall be reunited with them, but on a higher plane, experiencing a more radiant love than ever before, and the suffering we knew shall disappear in the twinkling of an eye.

We have made huge leaps in human consciousness in the last few decades. We are awakening to our higher selves, who know that what we do to this wonderful world, we do to ourselves. The indigenous people knew this intuitively, but we had to find out by experience, intellect and reason.

Indigenous people also knew the importance of the bereaved being part of their loved ones' transition from here to eternity. This is still acknowledged and continued in many ancient traditions, such as the wake in Celtic communities where people come together to "wake" the deceased: give a good send-off, telling stories in love, laughter and tears, and supporting those who grieve.

While the body is held in sacred space between Heaven and Earth, the spirit makes its journey to a higher vibration of light. Those bonded in life and bereaved may also start the journey of relinquishing their physical bonds to make way for a higher connection, creating bridges of light that will never be extinguished. As in life, as in death, love is the eternal expression of light in the evolution of human consciousness on our return journey to the oneness of all creation.

"Everything that has a
beginning has an end.
Make your peace with
that and all will be well."

—Buddha

From We to I

Reflections on Losing a Life Partner

Patricia

The death of a spouse or partner is one of the most shattering events a person will endure in their life. Life changes irrevocably, and the companionship of "we" becomes the aloneness of "I."

Each relationship differs, and each experience of loss naturally does too. Not all relationships are happy—most contain a mixture of good and bad. But as anyone who has suffered such a loss knows, you don't travel a long road with one significant person by your side and not experience a major life adjustment in the aftermath of their loss, along with a process of grief that is complex and deep.

I remember when my own mother died how worried we all were for our dad. My parents had been very lucky to have a warm and loving relationship for the fifty years they were married. In their later years, the woman who came once a week to clean for them told me she was fascinated that they still had so much to say to each other. "They're always talking away to each other, having their breakfast." That made me laugh, but it was the loss of my dad's soul mate that grieved me. We helped him on the path of loneliness, grief and heartache as much as we could but he, as with most widows and widowers, could only experience it alone.

Dad always loved music and listened to his CDs and tapes often. When my mother died, that stopped. The joy had gone out of him. But one day, about two years following her death, I was driving him home from an appointment when he started to hum a tune, then sang a few words of the song. I can't tell you how much my heart lifted at the sound. It was the first time in two long years that he had come back to himself a little. I couldn't wait to ring my sister and tell her that Dad was singing: it was a big step on his road forward.

Recently I spoke to a dear relative in her late seventies who was just over the first-year anniversary of her husband's death. They had worked together in their own business, reared a large family, then enjoyed retirement and their grandchildren together. She was devastated by his death. She told me how strange and difficult it was to refer to herself as "widowed," and how, despite her children, grandchildren, many other relatives and friends, she had never experienced such loneliness.

She's a positive woman, though, and brave, too. She told me that now the first anniversary was over, she had joined a swimming club, and started going for walks again with her walking club. She had also renewed her passport as she was "ready to travel again." She is now seventy-eight, having suffered the heart-breaking loss of her husband, and several siblings, but I am in awe of her positivity and determination to live life to the full. She is inspiring.

In this next piece, Mary Helen's lovely mother Helen writes with honesty about the experience of losing a beloved husband and life companion after six decades together. Helen is another living example of how, after the dark days of intense mourning, we can take up the reins of life again and, in a different way, live it to the full, if we allow ourselves to step beyond overwhelming grief.

Helen Hensley
The Gift of Life

"I understand." How many hundreds of times had I written these two words to friends who had lost husbands and wives. Their grief was shared, my sympathy and empathy were sincere, but the truth was, I *didn't* understand. I couldn't, because I had never experienced it myself.

That day came, after sixty years of marriage . . . then I understood. My experience is that the closer you have been in life, the easier it is to let them go in death; not that you don't miss them terribly, but memories and gratitude for the time together combine to push the grief aside.

Like fingerprints and DNA, no two deaths are exactly alike. A missionary nurse, who was the guest speaker at a church in Richmond, Virginia, caught everyone off guard by starting her talk with these words: "Everyone in my hospital dies." (Gasps from the audience.) Then, "And so will you . . . from mortality."

Alzheimer's is a little like that in that there is no cure. The waiting periods differ but, like a thief or robber, it steals the most precious gifts of everyone it touches—memories.

But my memories live on, and sustain me. From the time of our marriage in 1952, my husband, Dick Hensley, declared that he was a snow goose. That stemmed from the age-old belief that these majestic birds mate only once, for life. In 1982, as a reminder of this, he gave me a fifty-seven-page treasure. The little book was called The Snow Goose by Paul Gallico.

Inside the cover, Dick wrote, "I have loved and will only love once a mate. I am a Snow Goose."

My memories of good times together sustained me after he died in 2012. He had been suffering from Alzheimer's for several years by then. Much of what had defined our relationship over years and decades had ebbed away—but the sustaining love remained, right until the end. Along with happy memories.

Each of us has such memories—private and personal, known only to the hearts of those who created them.

For me, it has been healthy and healing to keep a sense of humour and a smile. You can withdraw those funny or precious moments from your memory bank at any time. Write them down!

I understand that everyone has their own way of dealing with death, particularly with that of a life partner. Humour was a key component of my sixty plus years with my husband. The following story is an example of how for me, humour "lightened the load" along the way.

When Dick was eventually moved to an Assisted Living facility, where his needs could be better met than at home, humorous moments were peppered throughout our daily challenges with Alzheimer's. Anyone who has ever dealt with this disease will understand what I mean. As sad as it is, an

Alzheimer's patient also has the capacity to say and do things that sometimes one simply can't help but laugh out loud at.

One day, one of the three around-the-clock sitters was ready to take Dick to the dining room for supper. The sitter started toward the wheelchair, when Dick's hand went up in a "STOP" position and the sitter was promptly sent out of the room. Dick said to me, "I want a pledge from you. Hold up your hand." And I did.

"I pledge I won't court." I pledged. "I pledge I won't date." I pledged. "I pledge I won't marry." I pledged. Knowing how much I loved to eat out, I cringed when I heard the next command. "And I pledge I won't eat out with another man." Mischief made me hesitate a second, but I pledged.

Once the "contract" had been sealed, in a rare moment where Dick seemed to be fully coherent and well able to speak without mumbling or at a loss for words, we made our way to the dining room. I pushed him to a table by the door. In walked an elderly, heavily whiskered gentleman for his supper. He glanced over at us and in a nonchalant way said, "Good evening." I said "Good evening" in return and with that, Dick banged his hand on the table and loudly proclaimed, "So much for your pledge!"

Dick, ever the Snow Goose!

I kept all of those pledges I made, not because I had to, but because, you see, I am a Snow Goose, too. On days when I am really missing him, I look back at funny little moments like these and am ever grateful that I can laugh and remember.

Memories of course do not stop the pain of grief, the sensation of missing someone. I sometimes dial my home phone from my cell phone just to hear Dick's deep voice and distinctive Southern accent, saying, "You have reached Helen and Dick Hensley. Sorry we've missed your call. Please leave your name and num-bah. Have a great day!" It brings a smile.

It has been over five years and it's great to hear "Coach" stories from family, friends, former players and students, the men's Thursday-morning Bible study group (which he taught), and from anyone with a memory to share.

Even in the midst of missing him, I have a constant grateful, joyful feeling for the sixty-plus years we had together. In the last days of Alzheimer's, Dick's favourite scripture was I Corinthians 13:13. "And now abide faith, hope, love, these three; but the greatest of these is love." Those words are on Dick's headstone.

The night before he died, I left his room for a quick trip to the pharmacy. The only other customer was a doctor friend, who immediately asked how Dick was. My face showed the answer. Then he asked, "Helen, have you told him that it's all right to go?" I nodded yes. He continued, "I mean have you told him tonight?" I shook my head, no. He simply said, "Tell him." And I did.

I received a call early the next morning: Dick had died peacefully.

The first person I encountered as I arrived at Dick's room was the young gentleman who had spent the late-night shift sitting with Dick. He had the most peaceful look, and needed to speak privately to me.

"I never knew what Mr Hensley looked like as a young man, but I know now. He looked radiant, youthful, and the beautiful lights around him filled the room." He felt so honoured to have witnessed this and told me it was a life-changing experience for him.

His words were the first of comfort to me, and the best. How special that this young man had also had a glimpse of Heaven.

In some situations where there have been long-term illnesses ending in death, the spouses have felt a sense of freedom following the loss. This often causes a feeling of guilt.

This is not freedom by choice, but created by loss. In my case, in well over a year with the progressing stages of Dick's Alzheimer's, I left town overnight only once. That was to accept Dick's induction into the University of Richmond Athletic Hall of Fame. How I wish his health had allowed him to be there with his family, friends and the former players he had coached. I had that pang of guilt for being away, but showing him his Hall of Fame award the following day was a special moment for all of us.

To the spouse or partner who is left behind, know that family and friends are there for you, wanting to help fill the gap. Please let them. It's their loss, too.

And, truthfully, there is a freedom of sorts, albeit one you didn't wish for. But it's one that comes with numerous possibilities to experience life in new and different ways. For me, it meant I could travel and visit each of our four children and their families in their homes in Florida, Virginia, North Carolina and Ireland; we hadn't been able to do that for years due to Dick's health.

Among other gifts, Dick gave flowers often, but once, many years ago, he picked a tiny blooming wild flower (or weed) from the lawn of Ashford Castle in Ireland and presented it to me with a great flourish. It remains pressed in my memory book to this day.

The early Japanese flower arrangers were noted for their beautiful floral creations, which were never judged because they were considered expressions of the soul, therefore impossible to judge. Grief expresses itself in different ways, so who are we to judge how another interprets this natural part of the human experience?

Each person has a God-given gift.

It might be the gift of speaking,

It might be the gift of listening,

It might be the gift of just being present.

But remember . . .

There's one gift we've all had or have in common.

The Gift of Life.

Aidan

The Other Half

In a long-term partnership, we come to experience our significant other as an integral part of ourselves. I certainly know that's how I feel about my husband Murtagh. With a marriage your lives become so intertwined that two often become one. People often expect you to be together wherever you are—you go somewhere alone and are asked, "Where is your other half?"

I deal regularly with clients who are in grief at the loss of a spouse or life partner. One thing I am told again and again by them is that they feel half of them is missing and that they don't fit in anymore. Their best friend is gone and they have no one to share their life with. They'll often tell me that no one understood or loved them like their partner did.

Most of their friends are couples and while it was once a great joy to share a friendship, before the death of their spouse, now it has become awkward. My clients often feel more alone going out with these friends, and have concluded that it is easier not to go out socialising at all.

The most common emotions clients share with me are loneliness, sadness, fear and anger at themselves, and at the spouse who has died. They are worn out, not able to think clearly or make decisions. They have no energy, and sometimes feel guilt. Strange as it may seem, these emotions are normal while dealing with grief.

As my angels have told me time and again, when coping with grief it is good to remember that your real friends are always there for you. Talking and resting are the keys to overcoming grief. Stay well away from people who tell you how you *should* be feeling, they will only upset you more. We all grieve differently.

I have also had clients who are relieved and yet guilty for feeling a sense of freedom when a spouse or life partner has died. The relationship has not been the best, and they have been confined in a bad marriage. They talk about how good it is to feel unhindered and alive again. They have felt trapped and controlled by their spouse for years, and now that the pain and fear has ended they can start a new life for themselves. My clients always wish it could have been different but they were trapped and didn't have the energy, the means, or the belief in themselves to walk away.

Again, if you are bereaved and in this situation, do talk about your feelings. You are not alone. People do understand more than you think. Feeling relief after a death does not make you a bad person. As the old saying goes, "There are two types of pain, one that hurts you and the other that changes you."

I had a lovely client that came to me one day. As she sat opposite me I could see the grief in her eyes. I asked her who she was grieving.

"My ex-husband," she said.

"When did he die?" I asked.

"He died six months ago and I feel very sad since he went. I feel so silly, to be honest," she admitted. "We were divorced and are living apart almost twenty years and we didn't have what you would call the friendliest relationship during that time. My children and friends can't understand why I am grieving."

"Did you love him?" I asked.

"Love is a strong word but yes I suppose I did. I just didn't like him or what he did to me during the bad times. He didn't treat me very well. We were married for almost twenty years and I suppose you don't forget that." She went on to tell of how she was madly in love with him when they first met and got married, and loved him up to the day he walked out on her twenty years ago.

Then, her love for him turned to hate, and eventually to indifference.

So she could not understand why she was so grief-stricken.

"Am I just silly?" she asked.

"No, you're not silly at all," I reassured her. "You loved him once and you are mourning for all the good times you had together. I feel you still loved him, but you were no longer *in* love with him. Maybe you are mourning all the good things that might have been," I said.

Grief has a funny way of hitting us, often when we least expect it. Love lies deep in the stillness of the heart and for most people the loss of a spouse is the greatest grief they will ever experience.

She seemed to take comfort in that idea, and told of how she had always loved him deep down. I could see the tension ease in her as she left feeling comforted, knowing that there was still a love of sorts between her and her deceased husband.

Grief, as I said before, has a funny way of hitting us, often when we least expect it. Love lies deep in the stillness of the heart and for most people the loss of a spouse is the greatest grief they will ever experience. But grief is not insurmountable, and the greatest gift we can give our loved one is to pick up the reins of our lives and move forward, giving thanks for the blessing of the relationship we had and knowing that they are just a thought away.

Affirmation for Healing the Trauma of Loss of a Life Partner

I recognise that grief is a necessary process
for healing the trauma of loss.
I surrender to my tears, they are my healing balm.
I take time to remember, cry
and reflect on our relationship,
and on the gifts that it bestowed.
[Give consideration to these.]
In memory, and in Spirit,
I connect to our everlasting love,
and remember that it is still with me.
In the name of our love, I undertake to take
one day at a time, being kind to myself,
not judging myself or setting unreasonable expectations,
but doing the best I can, one step at a time.

"Grieving the loss of a child is a process, it begins on the day your child passes and ends the day the parent joins them."

—B. J. Karrer

Forever in Our Hearts

Reflections on Losing a Child

Patricia

There is probably no loss greater than the death of a child. It feels as if it goes against the natural order of things and, as such, nature does not equip us to deal with it. For many parents and families, the wound will not heal. The devastation can feel complete.

No one can take away the pain that comes from loss of a love so profound it is hard to express it in words.

In this chapter, my co-authors would like to share with you their experiences and knowledge around such an event, from a Spiritual perspective. Our hope is that some solace can be found in knowing that a cherished child remains cherished and loved in the afterlife, and is never far away.

Aidan

An Angel's Embrace

This is an experience I had some years back, when I was out walking one evening. It was a devastating event, and the impact never left me . . . but what I saw in the aftermath was a vision so beautiful, and beyond anything I could ever have imagined, that it changed how I view death forever.

The incident involved the death of a child in a hit-and-run incident. That evening as I set out for my usual walk, the street was quiet, except for a few cars passing and the odd person out for a ramble, like myself. I had been walking for a while when suddenly, in the distance, I heard a thud and a screech of what sounded like car brakes.

Next I saw a blue van travelling at great speed about thirty metres ahead of me. There appeared to be something trapped beneath it as it continued to travel at high speed. It was swerving all over the road and I felt afraid. Aside from a car following the van, the street was empty.

I shouted at the driver to stop, but to no avail. A tiny bundle at last escaped from under the van and lay like a rag doll, limp and lifeless, on the side of the road. I began to run towards the injured child, and the couple driving behind the van stopped and ran to her aid. Next thing, I saw a *multitude* of angels gather around the spot where the child lay. I arrived to find the body of a small girl of about eight, with long blonde hair. She was still holding tightly her little bag of sweets.

The lady from the car held one of her small hands while I bent down and took the other. People began to gather around us asking questions, attending to the child, and screaming for an ambulance. I began to feel suffocated and had to step back. I was shaking and felt as if I was having an out-of-body experience. Nothing seemed real.

As I looked back at that beautiful child, I could see a gathering of angels, in great light, holding her. Then, behind her, this wonderfully strong, vibrant, purple light was shining and from that light the most beautiful angel emerged, shimmering in many colours. I stepped further back. I had never seen such powerful energy before or experienced such great gentleness and strength.

He appeared in that mighty beam of light, tall, youthful, bearded, and his radiant energy extended way beyond that of any other angel I had ever come in contact with. All the angels stepped aside for him as he made his way to the stricken child. He bent down, gently embraced the little girl and kissed her on both cheeks, first the right and then the left. Then he held her in his energy for a couple of minutes. Her own energy changed. The tension left her and she relaxed. The mighty angel took her hand and the Spirit of the child left her body, a shining white light radiating around her. He took her into his arms, stepped back into the beam of purple light and they slowly faded away.

"Who is that angel?" I asked my own angels, who had come to my aid. "I have never met his energy before." Even through my shock, I was in awe of what I was witnessing.

"This is the Divine-like energy you call Metatron. He protects and guides children in life and beyond. She is safe now," I was told. "The Archangel Metatron will take the Spirit of the child to a place of eternal love and light and perfect peace. Here, in the Crystal Temple, this perfect and precious child will be loved and cradled by the angels, and also by the soul family and relatives who have passed before her. Here, all fear and pain is instantly removed. Then she is placed in the loving care and energy of God."

"Why did she die so young, that beautiful child? It doesn't seem fair to me," I said.

"It was her time. She had learned all she came to learn and her death was her last lesson. She will need time to adjust now, as indeed will her loved ones here," Hannah, my guardian angel, replied gently.

Although Metatron had left with the Spirit and soul of the child, the other angels protected her body as we awaited the ambulance. The paramedics attended to her very carefully and with the greatest respect as they took her body to the hospital.

For days afterwards I was in deep shock. Although it was a terrible experience on a human level, it was inspirational to see the angels attend to that mortally injured child and stay with her, and also to witness the great gentleness and love of that powerful angel, Metatron. This gave me great comfort.

To see a young child die through reckless driving caused me to question my faith at a very deep level. How could such a thing happen? How could a loving God preside over such terrible tragedy?

All the while my angels reassured me that there is a Divine Plan to all our lives and everything happens for a reason, but it was difficult to accept. Yet I felt very privileged to be allowed to watch a soul making the transition from this Earthly dimension to the Heavenly Realms.

I've been present at more deaths since, and the experience is almost always the same. The Spirit and the soul embrace the light. They lift very gently from their Earthly body and their energy becomes relaxed and floats. I have seen a soul family come for a loved one, and most times, *they* take the hand of their relative first, while the angels lead them into a beautiful silver-white misty light. The departing soul never looks back. They always seem so happy to merge and slowly become absorbed into the misty light.

I've had many clients come to me because of a child's death, and have been able to reassure them without the shadow of a doubt, because I've seen it, that no matter what the circumstances of their dying they are never alone. Archangel Metatron has always been there, and always will be, to bring great comfort, gentleness and love at the moment of a child's passing. He or she is always happy to go into the light, holding his hand and never looking back.

Pamela

"O death, where is your victory? O death, where is your sting?"
—1 Corinthians 15:55

The sting of pain, loss and regret is inherent in the bereavement process, but where is the victory? It is in the abundant blessings and awakenings we may come to receive from those who have passed and those who remain.

We shall all be deeply affected by death, no matter how it appears in our life and with whom—and never more so than when it is the death of a child, someone whose life was only beginning.

The daughter of Joyce, one of my closest friends, died at the age of twenty-one. Isobel was born with congenital heart disease, but died from a brain haemorrhage.

Joyce and I met soon after Isobel's death, introduced by a woman who came briefly into both our lives, as if that was her purpose. We had an instant connection. Little did I know that within six months I, too, would suffer a great and sudden loss.

All my life I had accepted and experienced another realm in which "dead" people live. I simply shared my beliefs about life after death with Joyce and we started to meet for walks in nature, in meditation and in prayers, all dedicated to, and for, Isobel's short life. We immediately experienced a kinship, and even though I hadn't met Isobel I felt her presence, as did Joyce.

Six months after I'd met Joyce, my mum died suddenly, and although I knew where she had gone, I too was bereft and in deep mourning for the physical loss of her. Joyce was a godsend to me and I have no doubt we were brought together to help each other through our pain and move forward together on a new path of revelation. Death brought us a deep and loving friendship that led us along a shared journey, a beautiful and profound adventure into a much deeper Spiritual awareness.

We knew we were being led by our loved ones in Spirit. We felt their presence, their guidance and their love. Many times we heard, "And this, too, shall pass," and it is true, although we didn't think it would at the time.

When it did come to pass, though, we didn't want to let go of that which we felt kept us in touch. Albeit painful, the grief connected us with our loved ones.

Time healed, in spite of our perceptions, and eventually we let go of the longing for and loss of our physical bonds, and when we did, a new adventure of awakening appeared before us, applauded by our loved ones.

For the twenty-two years since the death of our loved ones Joyce and I have communed with a higher light that has guided us along a Spiritual path dedicated to uncovering our own inner light. For years we have sat with Brenda, another grandmother, in silence with the simple intention of sending our love out into the world for peace. We have walked in silent meditations in the countryside beneath the sacred trees as they breathe the breath of Goddess and God on Earth, giving balm to our grieving and love to the world. We call our nature walks "Walking the Druid Way."

We have attended inspiring Spiritual events wherever we could. We have experienced many healing and Spiritual modalities such as Reiki, Ho'oponopono and chanting. We have read, listened to talks, enjoyed sacred-circle dance and drummed.

We have greatly benefited from going to the Monastery in Manchester, which had fallen into ruin and had been rebuilt into a wonderful Temple of Light, which is now open to all. A venue of outstanding beauty for weddings, concerts and ceremonies, it is also a sacred space where we share knowledge and receive inspiration of all kinds. It is a powerful and miraculous place of awakening.

All these experiences led us to the most important blessing of all: that of going within and becoming self-aware. There is no turning back once we enter the path of Spiritual development where great joy and great challenges are brought to light. This path of awakening is the agony and the ecstasy that arise from the ego finally relinquishing to the higher self as we learn to let go of patterns that cause torment to us and our loved ones.

The ego is a great vehicle to enlightenment. We become aware that whatever we are experiencing is given as an opportunity for healing, that we should respond in love rather than react in fear. In this peaceful state of being we may come through and awaken to our true nature, that of an eternal being. In this state we have the opportunity to be at one with those in the realms of Spirit.

More and more people are going within, where the silent self of non-judgement awaits, the self that is unconditional love and light, where only pure awareness of who and what we really are exists.

The greatest gift of bereavement is to be opened up to this inner journey, an altered state engendered by death, ultimately experienced by those who pass to the world of Spirit, but which can also be a profound "knowing" by those who live on.

Since our bereavements, Joyce and I have been led by our loved ones in Spirit. We have felt their presence, their guidance and their love. As time healed, a new peace descended from which we were embraced by a new and radiant connection. We are on our unique journeys, travelling on parallel paths of love and light connections with our loved ones, until we meet again in the beautiful world awaiting us.

Joyce has kindly given me permission to share part of her story here, of losing Isobel. There is no grief like a parent's for their child.

Losing Isobel

A Mother's Story

Isobel Anne was born in 1972. She had a congenital heart defect and later in her teens was diagnosed with DiGeorge syndrome, which causes breathlessness, inability to walk any distance, learning, speech and feeding difficulties, hearing loss and poor immunity. Her early years were overshadowed by the possibility of her imminent death.

As a baby, she had feeding and sleep problems, and medical professionals pronounced that she would not survive beyond toddlerhood. Later, we were told she would not reach ten, then her teens, then no more than her teens, then beyond twenty-one. The final pronouncement almost came true. Isobel passed away aged twenty-one years, six months and three weeks.

Isobel's early days were fraught with regular hospital visits. When she was fifteen months old, we moved back to my hometown in the north of England to be near my family, as I was finding it hard to cope alone with Isobel's special needs.

The oxygen therapy that had saved her life as a baby damaged her brain, causing the learning difficulties, and she attended a special school. She was a giggly girl when she was well. Her life was limited but she was happy with her school friends, her little brother and extended family.

The last year of Isobel's life was difficult for us both. The college she was due to attend had lost her application and they had no places left. I was powerless and I felt her pain. Until something could be found she spent a lot of time alone as we were out working. She could see into her future and became depressed.

She was referred for a psychiatric assessment. I received a phone call to confirm an appointment on the day of her funeral. I think she gave up.

Months before Isobel's passing, I had started an aromatherapy and massage course where I made friends with a woman called Eileen. She and her husband were healers. When I told her about Isobel, she suggested I bring her to one of their healing circles. I put it off, but eventually, out of desperation, I went along with a reluctant Isobel.

It turned out to be the strangest Monday evening I had ever spent: I was out of my comfort zone and out of my depth. I didn't realise that the healing circle also included clairvoyant messages. A lady gave Isobel a message, saying she could see a parrot of beautiful colours and soft feathers fluffed up near her face. She was also told that she would get a wonderful surprise. We came out laughing, feeling joyful, and wondering what the surprise would be. Each day following that message, Isobel rang me at work saying she could feel the feathers on her cheek. It cheered her up but, to my shame, I dismissed it as her wonderful imagination.

On Friday night, 11 February 1994, Isobel became ill. In hospital they discovered she had had a sub-arachnoid brain haemorrhage and sedated her heavily to stop her fitting. From that moment, I never left the hospital or her side. The following day she was pronounced brain-dead. We were asked if Isobel would want to donate her organs. We agreed, and her body was kept alive until the transplant team came up from Birmingham.

On Sunday at noon, 13 February, they took my healthy-looking, pink-skinned, sleeping girl to the operating theatre.

Two hours later they returned her, white, waxy and gone.

The church where my children had gone to Sunday school years before heard about Isobel's death and asked to hold the funeral service. Two days before the funeral, my step-daughter, Jackie, who had shared a bedroom with Isobel, came downstairs looking overwrought, white and upset.

She had woken in the night and was terrified to see a light darting about the bedroom so fast she could hardly keep up with it. I felt jealous that I hadn't seen it and asked why she hadn't called us. She replied she had put her head under the covers, eyes tight shut, until she fell asleep. She was too afraid to sleep there any more so her dad and I swapped bedrooms with her.

On the first night we, too, saw a light in the bedroom and I was comforted.

It was after my local church told me that it represented evil Spirits in my house that my friend Alison suggested I meet Pamela Young, her work colleague, who might help me to cope with the turmoil I was experiencing. I was reluctant to take any more advice from strangers, even more so when Alison told me that Pam's mum was the president of the local Spiritualist church.

As soon as I met Pamela, relief swept over me. Not only did she look "normal," she was kind, gentle and caring too. We talked and talked into the night. Pamela's beliefs sat well with me. She gave me a book on Spiritual healing called Hands of Light by Barbara Brennan. I became fascinated with this and working with the pendulum, a practice of divining that promotes healing. I met Pamela's mother, a lovely lady, who welcomed me into her heart.

Many synchronicities had led me towards my awakening to something greater than I had known before. My life changed completely after my daughter's death—Spiritual meetings, meditation nights and attending the Rainbow Group, started by Pam's mum Evelyn, where we would take turns to create evenings of inspiration and creativity. We have attended mind, body, Spirit fairs and have been initiated into Reiki one, two and three. I couldn't afford to do the courses but I was told to trust. The universe answered my call and the money was given to me. It was miraculous, and I didn't have the words to explain it, but now I see that when we are ready to awaken we receive.

When I look back, I am amazed at how far I have come since I took my first steps on this path. I could not have done it without all the help I have received along the way from the people I have met for a reason, a season or a lifetime.

My Isobel's death has changed me dramatically but not in the way people might think. I have travelled the road of the bereaved mother, the sad, crying, lost soul, and believe me, it lasted for years. But alongside this, with Pamela's help and guidance, a Spiritual awakening I could never have imagined took place. The more I learned, the more I searched. I was introduced to the idea that you could commune with angels, Spirit guides and the Divine Feminine.

I gradually incorporated these practices into my life with meditation and Ho'oponopono, which helped me enormously. I looked into the old religions, and visited sacred sites and standing stones. My mind was expanding, and my beliefs totally changed as I became a different person.

I grieved for seven years. By year six the pain was more manageable. The seventh anniversary took me by surprise. I was more upset because I felt I was losing my connection with Isobel and I didn't want to—I felt she was moving on—but after that dip I began to feel better. I, too, was moving on.

In my previous life before Isobel passed, I would not have considered any of this. It would have seemed weird to me and to everyone else I knew. But now it is second nature and I am not concerned if my beliefs do not sit well with others. I am walking my own path—no approval needed!

I have come to a point where I believe that everyone has their time to die, be it from natural causes or accidents. Something has to take you at the right time. I feel we may even decide this before we are born on this planet. I received from Isobel that she was happy doing the things she had always wanted to do but couldn't do here on Earth. She told me she loved me and was glad that I had been her mum. She was and is ever-loving. From the bottom of my heart I hope I have made her proud.

So I thank you all, dear friends, but most of all I thank my daughter, Isobel, whose passing woke me up. I firmly believe that she arranged it before she came to this life. I owe her a great debt of gratitude. Where would I be now without her? I looked after her physical needs for most of her life and she has looked after my Spiritual needs. I thank her, secure in the knowledge that we will meet again.

Prayer for the Loss of a Child

Higher Power
Let comfort and peace come to all
who are grieving the loss of a child
With deep trust that understanding will transcend their grief.
We give thanks for the precious moments we
shared with those beautiful souls who have forever
changed us and left their footprints on our hearts.

"In life there is no
beginning nor end,
only experiences that
allow us to transcend."

—Mary Helen Hensley

Death Before Life

Reflections on the Unborn

Patricia

My co-authors and I share the belief that we come into this life with a "soul plan," agreed before our incarnation on Earth. This plan does not mean that every step is pre-destined, simply that we have agreed certain aspects of our lives in advance, in order to meet the challenges that can bring about the learning opportunities for this life, as we journey along its winding and sometimes unpredictable path.

There can be tremendous awe and wonder when we surrender to the recognition that while we may not be able to understand everything that happens to us or around us, in this lifetime, none of it is completely by chance.

I now believe that it was not part of my soul plan in this life to have children—much as I would have liked to. So I cannot claim to have walked in the footsteps of women who've experienced pregnancy, miscarriage, abortion, motherhood or the tragedy of losing a child. Instead I've been blessed with beautiful nieces and nephews, and now grand-nephews. I've helped their mothers through their pregnancies, and afterwards, and I've been present after two heart-breaking miscarriages, where the parents and I lit candles and surrounded the precious unborn child, who was returning to Source, and ourselves in love and light.

I felt very privileged to be there, and have no doubt whatsoever that both these precious souls returned when their mothers subsequently became pregnant again.

I believe that all souls choose to return to Earth to fulfil a Divine contract of learning and love. From the finest, highest, pure love energy that is the source of all, where we are one great consciousness of pure love, we travel downwards to become Earth bound. And sometimes that remarkable journey becomes overwhelming.

In her book *Hope Street* Pam tells of the vision she was given, showing how souls who are coming back to Earth are sung to their birth, through the dense layers of energy by the Mothers and Spirit guides who are always with them as they make their transition from the high energies of light to enter the wombs of their chosen mothers on Earth.

In this section, Mary Helen writes with her usual unflinching honesty and clarity about a painful and life-changing event she experienced as a young woman, and its impact on her work today, as well as providing insight into the soul's journey into the womb, and the difficulties that can arise. And Pam shares her own experience of miscarriage, her mother's experience of stillbirth, and the insights that came.

Mary Helen

Aggie's Story and a Personal Journey

Aggie came to see me after her daughters convinced their eighty-year-old mother that she needed assistance with her long-term chronic depression. Aggie had come into the city from her home in the country with great reluctance. Her daughters had a quick word with me before her session, explaining that for as long as either of them could remember, their mother had been surrounded by sadness.

Diagnosed years earlier with depression, Aggie took a sedative and an anti-depressant each day, as prescribed by her doctor. Concerned that their mother never seemed to get any better with medication, her girls wanted to explore the possibility that her "depression" might stem from something that no pill could ever fix.

When Aggie entered the healing room, I asked her if she knew why she had been brought to me. She laughed sheepishly, telling me that she had come only to appease her children. Next I asked if she had been told anything about what I do. "All they said was I needed to have an open mind because you weren't any ordinary doctor. They said you have some kind of powers or something."

The innocence of her country demeanour was both charming and heart-breaking. Once she had settled at the table, I began to hear the voices of my guides telling me what Aggie could not.

The story I "downloaded" concerned the source of Aggie's anguish and immediately brought tears to my eyes.

While holding her hand, I looked her in the eye, trying not to shock her too much with what I was about to say. It wasn't my words that would surprise her—she knew her story all too well, carrying its burden on her own for many years. I was conscious that this God-fearing Catholic woman would have to digest the fact that somehow I *knew* her darkest secret.

I relayed her blackest memory, stored so deeply in her cells, nearly word for word. The voice of my guides had not been mistaken.

Aggie had raised five children, the youngest of whom had just turned forty. Her husband had been a hard-working man by day and a hard-drinking man most nights. He was aggressive and demeaning towards Aggie; when he had drink taken his violent behaviour had often left her in fear for her children's safety, as well as her own. This hulk of a man berated Aggie for having so many children and threatened her with murder, if she ever got *herself* pregnant again. He was very matter-of-fact when he told her that he would kick her pregnant belly inside out, then wrap his hands around her throat and choke her to death if ever there was mention of another child on the way.

Aggie found herself in quite the dilemma in 1960s Northern Ireland. Her religion prevented her using birth control and her husband regularly raped her after a night out on the beer. When Aggie fell pregnant after just such an episode, she found herself with the heart-wrenching decision of choosing between her sixth baby's life and her own. Unable to contemplate what life would be like if her other five children were left without a mother, under their despicable father's care, Aggie fibbed to her husband: she told him she needed to make an emergency visit to her deathly ill sister in England for two days.

It wasn't just the baby that was aborted: any remnant of good humour or happiness Aggie possessed was left behind in the women's clinic in the UK, never to be seen again. She returned home a broken woman, pouring herself into caring for her children, but never with a smile, her heart always heavy with the guilt of her life-and-death decision. Her husband never found out.

She told no one, not friends, not even her sisters, and of course her children would never know the truth about her sadness.

Aggie stared up at me in utter disbelief as tears flowed down her cheeks. "How could you possibly know?" The unbearable grief was suddenly replaced by an unfamiliar sensation of relief: her liberation from pain after its source had been revealed, even if by a total stranger.

I took her hand and told her a different story. This time, the girl was only seventeen. She was just about to embark on the most exciting times of her life, having gone to visit a college that her parents had hoped she would attend in the autumn of 1987.

Never having taken a drink to speak of, she had succumbed to the merriment of a campus party and had become heavily intoxicated. When guided into an empty room by a boy who had been flirting with her all night, she soon realised that they were not alone. In an instant, two pairs of hands were tearing off her clothes, and her cries for help couldn't be heard over the loud music and laughter in the corridors of the dorm. Not only did she lose control of her safety and well-being that night, she lost her virginity as well.

Three months later, when other freshmen were deciding on classes and potential subject majors, this girl was deciding whether or not she could face the responsibility of carrying the baby inside her. She went on her own to terminate a pregnancy that would have taken her down a path she knew she was not meant to take. The choice was difficult but it was the right one for her. No one ever knew.

For three years, she masked the pain of her decision with smiles and laughter. She found solace in words that her father had once spoken to her, concerning a different situation that had been far less serious. "If you let continuous regret, remorse, self-persecution keep you from functioning now, if you persist indefinitely in feeling guilty and upset over something that is over, then you are behaving in a non-productive manner. Feeling guilty is not going to make your life any better. You can learn from this experience, and get on with living now." If only he knew just how valuable those words had been.

Three years later, a temporarily fatal car crash would find this girl in another world. Surrounded by an indescribable atmosphere of peace and knowing, she reviewed her life in the loving company of her Guardian Beings. She had the opportunity to explore the meaning of each and every decision she had ever made. Where there were gaps in her capacity to understand, her Guardians were there to enlighten her. Upon reaching the review of her eighteenth year on the planet, she received an in-depth explanation of what happens when a pregnancy is terminated, either by choice or by circumstances, such as miscarriage or even stillbirth.

She was privileged to witness how the incarnation of a soul operates, while she was out of the body, or "dead" as we like to say. First, bear in mind that we are souls incarnating in this realm (among many others) in order to have a human experience, not humans seeking to have a spiritual experience, as so many are taught to believe. We already are that which we seek. We are the Divine. Souls that are choosing to incarnate here have the option of entering this plane at the time of conception, any time during foetal development, with some opting to "slide" in just before the baby makes its way out.

Depending on what the soul feels that it requires to best accomplish what it has come to experience, the soul may temporarily occupy a growing foetus in order to gain a broader perspective of the mother's feelings during pregnancy. This has been scientifically/medically proven to translate and affect the foetal development and cellular memory storage of the mother's emotional state. This is also no different than the fact that a growing baby can be affected by chemicals ingested by the mother during various stages of pregnancy. There is learning to be had as a foetus if the soul chooses it. If the parent of the unborn child is going to terminate the pregnancy or if a physical challenge is going to prevent the child from carrying to term or being born alive, often no soul will incarnate at all.

She was shown that, in the perfect plan of life, if a baby is not going to be born, the soul who would have occupied the body of the child can *choose* to incarnate temporarily if it feels it can grow and learn from the experience in the womb. In turn, the soul may not occupy the body because the circumstances and resulting emotions are specifically and solely for the *individuals* responsible for the child's creation.

This is much like a car that is warming up on a frosty morning with its visible exhaust, wipers on, radio playing, giving all appearances of being "alive," yet there is no driver.

A body can grow physiologically inside the womb, yet a soul may not incarnate if the mother's soul plan includes a miscarriage, stillbirth or abortion. Either way, it's the choice of the *soul*.

The girl knew in that moment that she would use this information later to alleviate the suffering of countless others who had faced a similar situation.

Aggie sat at the table, her weathered hands trembling in mine. More than forty years had passed since she had sentenced herself to a lifetime of guilt and shame. "That girl was you, wasn't it?" She had the sweetest look of compassion as she gently squeezed my hands.

"Indeed, it was, Aggie. It's time to let yourself off the hook. You may be eighty, but while you still have breath in your body, you're never too old to learn something new. You didn't do anything wrong. That experience brought you to this very moment of understanding your soul's own plan. What's it going to be?"

Her smile radiated and was one of the most beautiful things I have ever seen. I reminded Aggie that in the grand scheme of life, there are no wasted moments. I did not want to see her swap her decades-old regret of terminating her pregnancy to save her own life for a new regret at having given away so many years to her suffering and pain. Her heartache had been real, and an important part of a story that would lead her to a new understanding in the winter of her life.

Time is irrelevant to a soul on a mission. When seeking to understand the inner workings of the human psyche and emotions, a soul thinks nothing about quantity when attempting to gain quality experiences. For me, it's moments like these that make me go home and drop to my knees in gratitude for every single thing that has ever happened in my life.

With hardship comes growth; with pain comes knowledge; with joy comes celebration. None of these is more important than another when gathering the threads that will weave the rich tapestry of a life worth living.

Pamela

The loss of a wanted pregnancy is always painful. It is a different kind of mourning—for a life we never knew yet carried inside us, and *knew* on some deeper level that seems to extend beyond words.

I was forty-two when I had a miscarriage. My children were grown and finding their way in the world. I was newly married to Simon and we decided to let Fate decide. A year later I was pregnant while working full time and doing a diploma in social work. Probably not sensible but we were thrilled. But it was not to be: a few weeks later I miscarried. We were terribly upset and disappointed. I so wanted Simon to experience being a parent.

As always, Mam supported me. She reminded me of the things that Spirit had shared with us in the sittings many years before, when she had experienced the grievous loss of her son Christopher, stillborn at eight months. They told us that babies who die before they take on human form in the womb return to the spirit world to become eternal flowers in the healing gardens, where their Spiritual essence gives forth their everlasting beauty and a fragrance.

People newly arrived in Spirit would be taken to these exquisite gardens, where they would be healed of their

Earthly scars by their communion with the beauty and fragrance of the flowers.

I was comforted to know that the seed of our love was an eternal, living essence, helping the departed to "come into their own," healed and living in their radiance, a testament to life and death on Earth.

A few years later we became grandparents to three lovely girls, who have brought us such joy and wonderful family times. Simon said that becoming a *grand*parent was the greatest gift he had ever received.

The Spirit friends informed us that if anyone was denied the wish to have a child on Earth, they could, when they passed over, become guardian mothers and fathers to children in the spirit world. They would all be in loving communion and walk with the bereaved parents on Earth, if the bond was healthy and loving.

The miracle of life.
The miracle of death.
The miracle of flowers.
The miracle of everything.

Standing Still Between Heaven and Earth: My Mother's Story

Mam thought she was well past the menopause when she found herself expecting at the age of fifty, with what was then called a "change baby." At first she was totally shocked and embarrassed, yet soon accepted this turn of events, and anticipated the new arrival with love and excitement.

When she was eight months pregnant, Mam was sitting at home when she felt her baby leave the Earth. It was as if the baby had fallen off a shelf in her womb, she said. She knew he had gone back to Spirit. The gynaecologist confirmed the baby had died. She would have to wait until she started in labour and give birth naturally to her deceased child.

We were all devastated. I don't know how my mother did it but she returned home until she started in labour. Although she mourned the loss of her baby, she had absolute faith in Spirit and in the knowledge that this profound experience was meant to be.

She sat with her physically dead baby in her womb for a month, but she also sat with his beautiful Spirit, which continued to grow in the spirit world. She saw him as a baby, alive and radiant in Spirit, being fed and nourished by love. When children die they grow up into adulthood in the children's realms, accompanied by the love and guidance of Spirit and angelic beings. Here they learn how to use their Divine imagination, experiencing exquisite colours, sounds, movement and music beyond our present perception on Earth. They may choose to bring this higher inspiration and enlightenment to their future incarnation(s) in their mission to co-create a higher light here that will help humanity make a leap in Spiritual consciousness.

A month later Mam gave birth to a fully formed beautiful little human being whom she named Christopher. She chose not to see his physical body. He walked with her from that day and grew into a pure and shining young man in Spirit. I have no doubt he was on the other side of the door waiting for her, arms outstretched, when she died.

As I write, I am crying with the love I feel for them and for the work of light they performed together in that month when they stood still between Heaven and Earth. I don't understand the esoteric details, but now I know intuitively that, during the month in which they let go of their physical bond, the relationship between Christopher and my mother became a sacred union, building a light connection between Heaven and Earth, joining the lower and higher frequencies, in service to "The Work." Whenever anyone connects in unconditional love we raise the vibration to create Heaven on Earth.

The one thing I am sure of now is that every love and every loss we experience will lead us into the light. Christopher was pure, uncontaminated by the lower frequencies here on Earth. As he evolved Spiritually, he was able to spread light to this realm through his guidance to and love for Mam. They are together now and continue their work, building bridges of light between the dimensions, as we all do unconsciously.

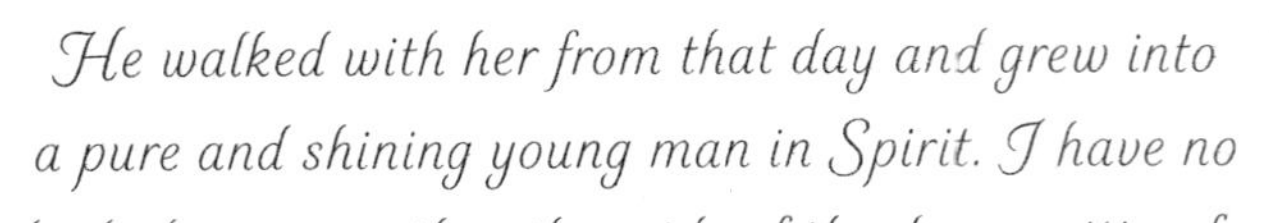

Aidan

Like Mary Helen, I have many clients who come to me distraught because of the death of a baby or a child. These sessions are always deeply moving, and invariably when they are finished and my clients have gone away in a more peaceful frame of mind than they came in, I give thanks that I am blessed to be a channel for the beautiful, comforting messages I am given by my angels and guides.

I am often asked about what happens to babies who have died before they were born. Other parents who have tragically lost a baby to Sudden Infant Death Syndrome invariably want to know about their child's Spirit. This is what I've been told by my angel guides.

A Message from the Angels

Before a soul is born, it meets its soul family (your family on Earth) and soul group (your friends, colleagues and others on Earth) on the great heavenly planes. Here they all plan their life together on Earth. Within this soul family, the infant soul chooses the parents they wish to be with, and every soul within that group decides the part they will play on that journey. They could present the soul with a difficult challenge, or be there to assist in ways of kindness and compassion.

There can be a number of reasons why a soul chooses to return to Heaven early, before it has a chance to be born. It could be that the young soul wants to experience a brief connection with their mother. It could be that they didn't feel they were ready to be born. Perhaps they haven't fully recovered from the trauma of their previous life. It could also be that they needed to bring the family closer together or to bring them to God/Spiritual awareness.

Always remember this precious and wonderful soul chose you to be their soul parents, so in time this soul will always return to you or the soul group. People often ask me why they can't become parents and I say to them that perhaps it's not to be your experience in this life. It doesn't mean you've never been a parent in another life. Tricia and I don't have children in this life but we are extremely close to our nieces and nephews and we know that in other lives we have had children.

Mothers, never blame yourself for a miscarriage. Even if you were to cover yourself in cotton wool and stay in bed for the duration of your pregnancy, this precious and perfect soul would still have chosen to leave and return to their heavenly home. There they recover and become whole again. In many cases this soul will return to the same soul parents, or if not, to the same soul family. It's important to remember it's the soul that returns, not the body. The soul is immortal.

An angel in the Book of Life wrote down my child's birth.
And whispered as she closed the book, "Too beautiful for Earth."
—Author unknown

"Let them think what they liked, but I didn't mean to drown myself. I meant to swim till I sank—but that's not the same thing."

—From *The Secret Sharer*
by Joseph Conrad

Bridge Over Troubled Waters

Reflections on Suicide

Patricia

Although, thankfully, we now live in a time where the taboo of suicide is not what it once was, it remains a subject that can be difficult for people to explore. Affected families not only have to grapple with the "ordinary" grief of loss, but also the more complex issues and emotions that can arise from losing a loved one in this way.

Not only is there the heartache of loss, and the shock of the brutal way of passing, but in many cases, for those left behind, there can be tremendous guilt.

Was there something more I could have done?

Could I have prevented this?

Is it my fault?

The torment is always there.

There can be anger towards the person who has taken their life for the anguish their death has caused. To find closure and healing after a death by suicide is very difficult, but with help and knowledge, the burden can be eased. Ultimately, healing can come, especially if the relatives feel they can connect with the loved one who has passed.

In this chapter, Aidan, Pam and Mary Helen share stories from their Spiritual work, helping relatives of those who have passed over by taking their own lives.

As they show, the message is always the same: there is no judgement and all who die in this way are met with great love and kindness.

Although I have never lost a loved one to suicide, I have known on a personal level what it feels like to contemplate it. I believe this is true for many of us at some point in our lives, or at various points—whether as a serious proposition or as something we muse upon in difficult times. When we're in real pain and hardship, it's natural to want to be out of the situation that is causing it. I experienced this in my mid-twenties, and I was in a dark place.

For years I had endured excruciating physical pain, which had begun when I first got my period at the age of twelve. Over the years, I was told variously by male gynaecologists that it was psychosomatic, that I had a low pain threshold, that I needed to eat more fibre, have a baby—you name it. No one, it seemed, could help me.

I struggled to get through secondary school—which I loved—and, when I was older, to manage at work. The general consensus was that women had to put up with painful periods. Finally a doctor sent me to a renowned surgeon who concluded that my appendix must come out.

I still remember him standing beside my hospital bed after the operation, shaking his head and saying, "I have so many young women coming to me in excruciating pain and when I open them up to take out their appendix it's perfectly healthy, just like yours."

My heart sank. If that famous surgeon couldn't find out what was wrong with me, maybe people were right—maybe the pain was all in my mind. I felt despair. I couldn't understand why, if I had created the pain and sickness in my imagination, I could not imagine myself well. I felt a complete and utter hypochondriac.

So began the years of psychological trauma and despair that accompanied the physical suffering before I was finally diagnosed with endometriosis. I remember the absolute relief of knowing I wasn't mad and hadn't imagined myself sick, that I had something with a name, even if it was hard to pronounce.

I was treated with drugs and got on with my life. I discovered the then recently formed Endometriosis Association of Ireland. The relief of meeting other people who suffered as I had! It had a life-changing effect on me. To be able to talk to people who knew of the wretchedness of endometriosis was as important to me as the medical treatment I was receiving. I wasn't cured by any means, I still struggled with my health, but at least I knew why I felt as I did.

Many times, though, before my diagnosis, I was on my knees in despair.

At the worst of those times, I contemplated suicide. I couldn't endure a lifetime of misery and pain. I resorted to stealing my elderly aunt's Valium, a couple here, a couple there, during every visit to her. I eventually had a stash that I felt would be sufficient. I'd even decided I wouldn't swallow them all because I'd read somewhere that people vomited after taking so many, and if I did that, there wouldn't be enough of the drug in my system to kill me. I planned to crush them along with a Crunchie, then wash the mixture down with alcohol.

Knowing I had a secret stash of drugs gave me great comfort. They were there, like a safety net, if I couldn't continue. In a perverse way that knowledge gave me the strength to put one foot in front of the other and keep going.

No one realised the depths of what I was going through because I kept my mental wretchedness to myself, enduring many dark nights of the soul. People would have been shocked to know this, because the part of me I presented, in essence the "real" me, loved life and enjoyed having good times with my friends and family.

When I hear of a suicide, I know the person who took their life tried their very best to endure, but it all became too much, and I think: there, but for the grace of God, go I or *any* of us.

Now having acquired wisdom, and Spiritual knowledge, I know that death by suicide is simply another form of passing, and as Mary Helen and Aidan will explain, sometimes an "agreed" form of transitioning.

There is no judgement, no dark place where the souls of those who take this step go. We all return to our Source. And if we so wish, we may return to live on Earth another time.

To those who grieve the loss of a loved one by suicide, I send empathy and love. Please know that in time you and your loved one will be reunited when your own time comes to pass, when you will see that the Divine Plan of all our lives is beautiful, no matter what our experiences. Those experiences are limitless. We have free will, and to those who grieve a loved one because of death by suicide, try to understand that it was not a selfish act, but an act of desperation when the struggle to keep going became too hard. It was not because of anything you did or didn't do, so do not blame yourself for the soul journey of another.

It is important to talk with those you trust, about your feelings, and your pain—to share what needs to be shared. You deserve to be heard, and held in your sorrow by those who love and care for you.

Mary Helen describes the process of understanding suicide from the point of view of a young child left behind by his father, and how our natural urge to shield children from the truth in such circumstances, while understandable, is not always the best solution to their pain.

Aidan's session with a grieving mother shows that while she is still devastated, knowing the whys and wherefores of her son's death has brought some peace of mind.

Mary Helen
Revelations from an NDE

Since my near-death experience, certain subject matter tends to attract itself into my experience, much like two magnets, which give the initial appearance of resistance when placed in close proximity yet inevitably snap together, refusing to let go.

With the tremendous privilege of precise recol-lection of every morsel of my NDE, I had the great blessing of witnessing what happens when a soul decides to leave the Earth encounter, either at the end of the soul's plan or after a single overwhelming event, or series of such, followed by a hair-splitting instant in which the decision to end the life was carried out. What I learned in this "space between lives" was that, in essence, there are two ways to die via suicide.

There is the "soul-plan" suicide. Here, members of a soul group or soul family will incarnate together and play various parts in one another's lives to assist in the ultimate growth and deeper opportunity to "know thyself" in human form. While the soul who agrees to exit via suicide doesn't necessarily consciously know their mode of exit, soul-plan suicides will often have quite incredible stories attached to them. For instance, the individual may say they know they will die before a certain age.

Rarely does a soul-plan suicide threaten to end the life and not follow through. Often, these deaths come as a complete shock to certain family members, as there were no apparent "signs," while other loved ones may report they knew "in their bones" that the life would end in tragedy.

From a Spiritual perspective, I was shown at the time of my own death that these soul-plan suicides carry no karmic ramifications. In the eyes of the Divine, it is simply one soul leaving an Earthly incarnation in a manner that will have a tremendous impact on the evolution and progression of the souls affected by the death.

When these souls pass, they move into the frequency of love where they are bathed in the music of the spheres until they are whole again. It's like washing off the grime of a marathon. You can't run the race without picking up some dirt along the way. The frequencies of the space between lives cleanse and renew, just like a long and glorious shower after an intense workout.

The other form of suicide I was shown was that which occurs as a result of overwhelm. The soul comes to the planet with a full life plan intact, with the aim to experience X, Y and Z while incarnate before departing by death in one of the more traditional exits, via illness or injury.

Somewhere along the line, the individual is overcome by an overwhelming feeling of darkness, leading them to believe that the only way to end the despair is by death. We will often hear news of these deaths and not be surprised. That's not to say every case is the same, but quite often the person who has taken their life in such circumstances has been thinking or talking about suicide for quite some time.

There can be failed attempts, self-harming and cries for help. Sometimes these individuals have regret as their last living memory: the bleakest feelings overtook them in the moment but really they wanted to live. They cut too deep, they tried to escape the noose but failed, they lost consciousness before they could throw up all of the tablets or a trembling finger on the trigger caused the gun to engage.

I was clearly and purposefully shown what happens in the aftermath of these cases. They move into the frequency of love, bathe in the music of the spheres, return to their Divine state of being and often opt to return to a new life in the Earthly realm, under different circumstances, with different players in a different environment, then recreate the feelings that brought them to death previously, in order to experience choosing differently. It is an incredibly thoughtful course of action taken by an eternal, omnipotent and loving soul in order to better know itself.

Despite what religious doctrine traditionally suggested, in its polarised ideas of Heaven and Hell, in reality only love, never Divine retribution, is in wait for a person who has taken their own life.

During my years as a doctor and metaphysical healer, I have worked with a staggering number of suicide-related stories. I do believe with all of my heart that nothing is without reason, and while it may cause me great pain, or I may not always understand it, the Divine is *always* in control, not just when it feels good or suits my agenda. This is a Universal law that applies to us all.

Of the many suicide stories I could share with you, with examples of both soul plan and overwhelm, I have opted to take a different approach. This is the story of a young boy, Michael, who had lost his father to suicide, and the path of healing for the child and his mother in the wake of this devastating event.

Those Who Are Left Behind—One Family's Story

Michael's mother Imelda wanted me to share their experience, from her perspective, in the hope that it might help others. She said, people need to know that there is no shame in losing someone to suicide. "I want people to know our story and that the only way we began to heal as a family was when we started talking about it ourselves."

Imelda first met her partner in September 2008. He was handsome, "talked the talk," as she put it, and had a very attractive confidence about him. What Imelda didn't know was that her perfect Mr Right was a Jekyll and Hyde character. Behind the façade of confidence and trustworthiness he led a double life: addicted to heroin, smoking cannabis, drinking alcohol, he took an extensive list of other drugs, including pharmaceuticals. Imelda was already in love with a man who would eventually become verbally abusive, completely unreliable and the bane of her existence.

"I want people to know our story and that the only way we began to heal as a family was when we started talking about it ourselves."

When Imelda was four months pregnant with their child, her partner left her and she didn't hear another word from him until their son was a week old. His dad first held baby Michael when he was two months old but declared he wanted no part in the baby's life and left the scene for nearly two years. Then Michael's father tried to be a dad but soon became unreliable again and wrote a letter to Imelda saying he wasn't able for a toddler in his life.

In September 2013, Michael's father got in touch just after Michael had started school at the age of four. According to Imelda, he did well as a dad for a few months, until the mood swings returned and he started picking fights out of thin air. He also came down quite hard on little Michael, accusing him of being hyperactive, even telling him he had ADHD. Imelda tried to explain that, at the age of four, Michael was so excited when his dad came to pick him up from school that he would try to tell him everything in the space of five minutes. The accusations of bad parenting began flying at Imelda and what had promised to be a two-parent life for Michael quickly turned into anxiety-laden trips to his father every second weekend. Imelda would have to collect him early because his dad was becoming enraged.

Michael's father was eventually sectioned in a psychiatric hospital in December 2015 and the following March he was released. The day after his release, he hanged himself in the shed at the back of his house, where he was found by two neighbours.

Imelda was at a loss when young Michael wanted to know how his father had died. She had opted not to tell him about the suicide because of his age. His anxiety increased, he became angry and upset at the slightest little thing and, to make matters worse, Imelda's own father had died the previous year. Michael was now beside himself: maybe his mother would die as well as his father and grandfather. All he could see was death all around him.

Eventually, a family therapist felt that it was in Michael's best interest to be told how his father had died, so that he could distinguish between his grandfather's death, due to natural causes, and his father's death by suicide. They hoped that this would calm his fear that his mother would suddenly drop dead.

Although Michael took exceptionally well the news about the way in which his father had passed, he remained very troubled, even aggressive, which worried Imelda. He was nothing like the well-adjusted and happy little lad he had been prior to his father's passing.

While it would have been easy to assume that this was solely the cause of his anxiety, Imelda suspected that something else was causing him to lash out. It was then that she decided to bring him to me, hoping that I could bypass his silence about the source of the aggressive behaviour and bring the child some peace. This is where being clairvoyant is a real plus. Often with children or, for that matter, with adults who are unwilling or unable to open up, the ability to see deep into another human to get a feel for their biography can really come in handy.

Within minutes, I realised that Michael was scared and angry simultaneously because only one of his major questions had been answered. He had been told that his father had taken his own life, but Michael's mind reeled at the thought of how he had done it and who had found him.

Understandably, the grown-ups had decided that this wasn't information he needed to know, but it had inadvertently led him to conjure a scenario that was driving him to distraction. He had imagined that his dad had thrown himself into the river and was dragged out by strangers.

I asked Imelda for permission to tell Michael the truth. He was thoughtful as he listened, asked a few questions, then said he was done. "Done?" I asked.

"That's all I ever really wanted to know. Daddy had a mental illness that took over his mind. That's why he did it. It wasn't because he wanted to leave me. He did this because he was sick. He actually loved me, didn't he? I knew it would upset my mother and she would cry if I asked what really happened, but not knowing was making me feel so angry."

Imelda had been trying to spare him the details and Michael was trying to spare Imelda the pain of having to tell him. In the end, they were both suffering.

While discretion and the best interest of the child was always the primary focus, in this case the truth set the child free.

Following our session, Imelda reported an immediate change in Michael. Not long after, I saw a post on social media of the most precious memorial garden Michael had built for his dad. He's no longer worried or agitated and is back to the carefree, loving child he was prior to his father's death.

This soul-plan suicide had served its purpose in Imelda and Michael's life. The potential to blame, carry shame, raise the child in terror of death and teaching him to fear the truth rather than face it was erased. Imelda and Michael took on one of life's most challenging issues and walked through the storm together. Imelda says that she and Michael have an unshakeable bond built on trust and mutual understanding, not only of the pain and grief caused by the suicide, but of the inner strength they have helped one another develop and the compassionate people they have become because of it.

Imelda shared with me that not only had the truth set Michael free but a deep-rooted wound in her own life had healed. When her mother died of breast cancer, Imelda and her eleven siblings had each been sat down by an aunt when they got home from school. Imelda said that she was handed a bag of sweets and told that her precious mother had been taken to Heaven to clean God's house. Bewildered that her mother was now God's housekeeper, Imelda grew up hating God.

Her partner's death had created the opportunity to change how her son would come to understand death. In the process, her own heart was healed.

Aidan

"Death is not the end! The exit for the world of mortals is the entrance to the world of immortals!" —Ernest Agyemang Yeboah

I love this quote and share it with you, dear reader, to remind you that when we leave this world a far better place awaits us, no matter how we pass. Like Mary Helen, I see many clients who have been touched by the horror of suicide, and while it's never easy, those sessions, no matter how difficult for the client and me, always bring healing. Because with knowledge comes peace. The session I speak about next is one of the most powerful I ever experienced and David's story will confirm what Mary Helen says: that suicide is sometimes part of the soul plan in this life.

Mary's Story—A Message from the Angels

Mary was my last client at the end of a busy day. I greeted her at the gate, offering her a hug as I often did to clients, but she didn't respond. I could see a grey energy all around her, her eyes were sad, and she seemed detached, unengaged. Her grey complexion matched the greyness of the day, and although I did not know the nature of her visit, I could feel her grief, which enveloped me in sadness too.

Mary was an attractive woman, in her late forties, but the pain in her face made her look much older. Was she okay? I enquired. Had she got lost on the way? I live in a remote spot of the Curragh of Kildare. No, she had found the place easily. We walked down the path to my room, in silence.

Once inside we sat facing each other, and I asked her to give me her hands so I could connect with her energy. She placed her cold hands on top of mine and, not for the first time that day, a shiver ran down my spine. The pain in her body and the weight of her hands almost floored me, but the pain in her heart took my breath away. I knew instantly she was grieving a very recent loss.

"What would you like me to look at, Mary?" I asked. "What do you want the angels to help you with?"

"You don't know?" she said crossly, almost snapping my head off. Her anger was almost palpable.

"Well, I do know you're in very deep grief and your heart is broken. You are very angry with the world and with God," I answered calmly.

"Anger doesn't begin to describe what I'm feeling—there are no words to express how I feel. As for God! I'm not sure about that either. You are my last hope. I need answers."

"What do you want me to do?"

"I want you to contact my beautiful son. God took him from us a few weeks ago and I need to know he is okay."

I looked at her in silence for a few moments. Tears were running down her cheeks. What could I say? My heart was racing. How could I explain that I wasn't a medium? I didn't want to disappoint her—she was in so much pain. I called on all my angels to guide me and help me to clarify this gently for her.

Hannah, one of my guardian angels, as usual came to my rescue. "Tell her the truth," she said. "We will guide you."

"Mary, I just want to clarify one thing," I explained. "I'm not a medium. I don't always communicate with souls who have crossed over, unless they come during my healings."

People come to me for direction in their life, and the angels help them on their path. "I also think it may be too soon for you to try to make contact with your son. Souls that have passed need time to adjust to the other side and to recover from the trauma of this life. I feel you should leave it a bit longer and give yourself and him some time to heal."

"I know you can help me," she said, "I found your book in his room and I know he directed me here. Please ask your angels to help me. Please," she implored.

"Of course I will," I assured her, "but I can't promise you anything. What was your son's name?"

"David."

The minute she said his name Hannah put her hand on my shoulder. I felt tightness around my throat and my breath went.

"He died suddenly," I said. "Was it suicide? Did he hang himself?"

I was inwardly shaking as I asked her this question, apprehensive about her answer, although I knew what it would be.

"Yes, in a field not far from our house." Her voice cracked and more tears filled her eyes.

"He was a gentle boy and loved his own company," I said.

"Yes, I lost my beautiful son. My blue-eyed boy. He had just turned seventeen, a gentle boy who was loved by his family and by most people—except for those bullies in school. He never told us about them, you see. If he had we could have done something about it. He left us a letter and told us he couldn't take it any more. They were killing him inside, he said." "Was he depressed?" I asked. "Was he on anti-depressants?"

"Yes, but he told us it was because he was so worried about his Leaving Cert and felt he couldn't cope. We took him to the doctor and he put him on a mild anti-depressant and it seemed to help. He seemed more relaxed and back to himself."

"Do you know what they were bullying him about?"

"Yes, but I need you to verify this for me and then I will know it's him, because no one else knows what he told us in the letter."

"I told you before, Mary, I can't promise you anything. I do hope he comes and maybe gives you some comfort and some peace of mind."

"Peace of mind! I doubt I'll ever have that again. I'm now on anti-depressants just to help me get out of bed in the morning. I don't see any reason to live any more. It's just not normal for a parent to grieve at their child's grave," she said.

"No, it's not." That was all I could say to this bereft, anguished mother.

"His poor father found him hanging from the tree in the early morning. He can't talk about it—or David. He just goes to work and comes home and sits in silence. He doesn't want to talk, or see anyone. We live in silence with this horrible loss—we're missing him so much. The house is eerily quiet and empty. People try to help but they can't—they don't understand our pain." She stopped and wiped her eyes as her tears overflowed.

Just then I felt a new presence in the room: it was a young male energy. Please, God, I said silently, let it be David. I looked at Hannah and she gave me the yes signal. She told me to say nothing for a few minutes. His energy needed to get stronger first.

Mary spoke again but her words choked her. "He was our only child. We felt so blessed when God sent him. He filled our life with joy and made us a family. All we have left now are pictures and memories."

I just looked at her and for the first time she met my eyes, and said, "You have the same eyes as my beautiful David," and she gave my hand a little squeeze.

I could see into her soul and it was so sad and empty. "I wish I could take this pain away from you, Mary. I wish David could come back. Keep him in your heart and talk to him every minute of every day and you will keep his Spirit alive," I urged.

At that, a beautiful scent filled the room.

"He is here. I can smell him! It's his aftershave—CK1!" she exclaimed. Her face lit up and she smiled for the first time since she'd arrived. Then she seemed to doubt herself, and her energy dropped again. She asked, "Are you wearing CK1? Is it you I'm smelling?"

"No, I haven't worn that for years, and I can assure you I don't have a bottle of it anywhere in the room," I said.

"It *is* David," she said. "It was his one and only aftershave and he loved it—he overdid it a bit most times." She gave a small laugh.

"Yes, he is here," I confirmed for her. "The angels have told me so. His energy is still a little weak. What do you want to know?"

"Is he happy and is he safe?"

"Yes, Mum. I'm happy and very safe, and Granny is with me!" David communicated through me.

"We miss you so much. Why did you do this to us, son?" Mary asked sorrowfully.

"I didn't do it to hurt anyone, Mum. I needed to kill the pain," David explained.

"Did you feel pain, son, when you hanged yourself? Were you all alone?" She was desperate to know the truth.

"I didn't feel any pain when I passed and Granny took my hand and brought me to the light, and the angels guided us. My passing was painless and peaceful. So please stop worrying about this. I am at peace, Mum," David urged his distraught mother.

Mary gave a deep sigh. "That's some comfort, because all I can think about is you in that cold field, in the dark all alone, not knowing what to do and being afraid." The words tumbled out of her in a rush.

"It wasn't like that at all, Mum. Truthfully, my soul had left my body days before that night, and all I was left with was an empty shell. I was lost in a world I didn't want to be in any more but tried to hold on for you and Dad. I was in a kind of limbo. I was straddling two very different worlds. I was barely coping. I could see and hear everything but I felt no connection to my Earthly home. I just kept seeing this beautiful light when I closed my eyes, and in my sleep I connected with it. I could see many family members who had passed and how happy they were. So, when I made my decision to go, I was happy and very peaceful and felt no pain at all, only joy. I'm so sorry you and Dad are so unhappy and I'm sorry for causing you so much pain. I do love you both and I will always be with you."

"But how could you leave us if you loved us so much, David? I don't understand." Mary shook her head, bemused.

"It was my time to go. I had learned everything I needed to learn in that life, and it was a wonderful life you gave me. I had everything I ever wanted. You are such good parents. God called me and I had to come. This is not something you will understand fully on Earth. But come the day when

I take your hand and lead you to the light you will see and understand why."

"I'll never get over this and nor will your father. How can we go on without you?" Mary still could not take in all her son was telling her.

"Life will go on, Mum, and everything will get easier. You are right that nothing will ever be the same for you and Dad but you will learn to live a different life and, if you allow it, in time, joy and happiness will return to you both. You will remember all the happy times we had together and not only dwell on my death. I am so glad I chose you as my parents and God allowed me to spend such a wonderful life with you."

"My darling son, I'm so happy you came into our lives and I'm happy to have had you, if only for a short time, rather than never have had you at all. I will always love you," Mary assured him tearfully.

"I have to go now, Mum. I'm getting tired. By the way, Aidan knows I'm gay. The aftershave was a giveaway. Be happy, Mum. That's what I want to see when I am around you, and tell Dad I love him."

She laughed and cried at the same time as she blew him a kiss.

"Thank you, Aidan," she said afterwards, "for your honesty and your kindness. I knew he would come to you. I now know he is at peace and safe."

"No need for thanks, but can I ask you a question?"

"Yes, of course," she said with a faint smile.

"Was he bullied at school because he was gay?"

"Yes, that's what he told us in his letter."

I gave Mary a big hug as she left, still broken-hearted but at peace, and thanked my angel Hannah for all her help with the session.

As you can see, David went to the light. It was his time and, as Mary Helen confirms in her segment, there is no punishment, no banishment to "Hell" for those who take their own lives. As Pam explains, in the vision her mother was given, each soul is eased into their new circumstances with love and kindness, especially if the transition has been difficult.

Everyone who dies, no matter how the "death" occurs, goes to the light whence they came. And that is all that matters.

Pamela

Forgive the person. Forgive yourself and live your life as best you can.

Advice from a sister who lost her brother to suicide

While we may have the deepest empathy with people who are bereaved through suicide, we can never truly know the pain, the trauma or the utter shock, which may last for years and sometimes a lifetime.

I had been told by my mother, who communed with Spirit, that there was great sadness when someone took their own life, but that always there was great love and understanding for them, too, and that they would be embraced by unconditional love and healing in the spirit world. Some who passed, however, were in such deep depression and mental turmoil that they continued in this state, unable to perceive the Spirits and angels who were waiting for them, until they became aware of the great love and light radiating their very being. Time in the human sense does not exist in the world of Spirit but when these Spirits started to awaken from their reverie, they were taken to the Golden Dome where people traumatised by life and death were placed in a state of deep healing surrounded by healing Spirits, colour and sound, until they were ready to emerge, unencumbered by their Earthly cares.

For the loved ones who are left behind, however, there is little understanding, apart from support groups. In fact, it is such a sensitive subject that often people would rather not mention the circumstances of a sudden death. But always the guides and angels helping the person who has died to "come through" the trauma will also surround the bereaved.

Often those who have taken their life return to heal the trauma experienced by their loved ones, as we can see from Aidan's beautiful story of David.

My own family has experienced suicide. I was young when my aunt and her boyfriend took their lives together sixty years ago. I don't recall much from the time, but I do remember the door being shut on a journalist who had come to pry. I remember the many discussions and the utter remorse of the relatives left behind. I remember going with my grandma on the bus and walking along a road just the week before, looking for the young runaway couple who were in love but felt there would be disapproval of their relationship. I remember the overwhelming sadness, the blaming and, of course, the "if only."

The two families were devastated at the tragic loss of two youngsters who'd had their whole lives ahead of them. Nowadays things would be different, and the couple might never have resorted to such a tragic ending. And in those days, suicide was something to be hidden and rarely talked about.

In later years I asked my mam if she'd had any contact with my aunt since she'd passed over. She had, and said that she was happy in the spirit world learning lots of things, and still dancing. She didn't want to return, unlike her young man who had already come back to learn the lessons he had missed in his previous lifetime. As Mary Helen says, every soul plan has a purpose—so who are we to try to second-guess the journey of another?

A friend of mine talked about her life following her brother's death, and the impact it had on her. She was a young woman when she found him dead—he had hanged himself. It took my friend fifteen long years to come to terms with it. Now, thirty years later, it seems almost unreal, a lifetime ago, and the details are blurred: she had made a conscious effort to let go and focus on the positive memories of her brother. She felt, too, that it was unhealthy to keep going over those painful events and reliving them.

She never avoided talking about her brother or about suicide, but on the rare occasion that the subject came up, she felt she was upsetting or burdening others, making them feel awkward. As Mary Helen noted, from her session with Michael, many families feel the need to protect others, especially children, from the details of suicide. It was often strangers who enquired if she had any siblings and, out of loyalty to her brother, my friend didn't want to discuss his death in a dramatic or tabloid-style way. Other than with family, she rarely talks about how he died, unless it is to help someone.

For two years after his death, she was deeply affected both physically and mentally by grief and the unanswered questions: her brother had left no letter or given any indication as to why he had ended his life. She is philosophical now, recognising that it was a life-changing experience, but also that every experience in life changes you.

Within a year of her brother's death, my friend suffered no less than four more close bereavements. She now views these experiences as massive life lessons. Having come through them, with the great love and support of her husband, her thought now is, forgive the person. Forgive yourself and live your life as best you can.

We can embrace a new age of understanding the Spiritual aspect of soul journey in suicide and be comforted in the knowledge that there is no judgement, and that often these souls come back to try again and learn what we must all learn ultimately: we are all one, and love is all that matters.

Prayer from the Angels for Those Coping with Loss from Suicide

Divine Source of Love and Light
welcome into your arms
All who have died by suicide.
Grant them peace from their inner
turmoil and the compassion of your love.
Comfort us who mourn their loss.
Support us in our sorrow and pain.
Help and comfort us in our grief and help us to find peace.

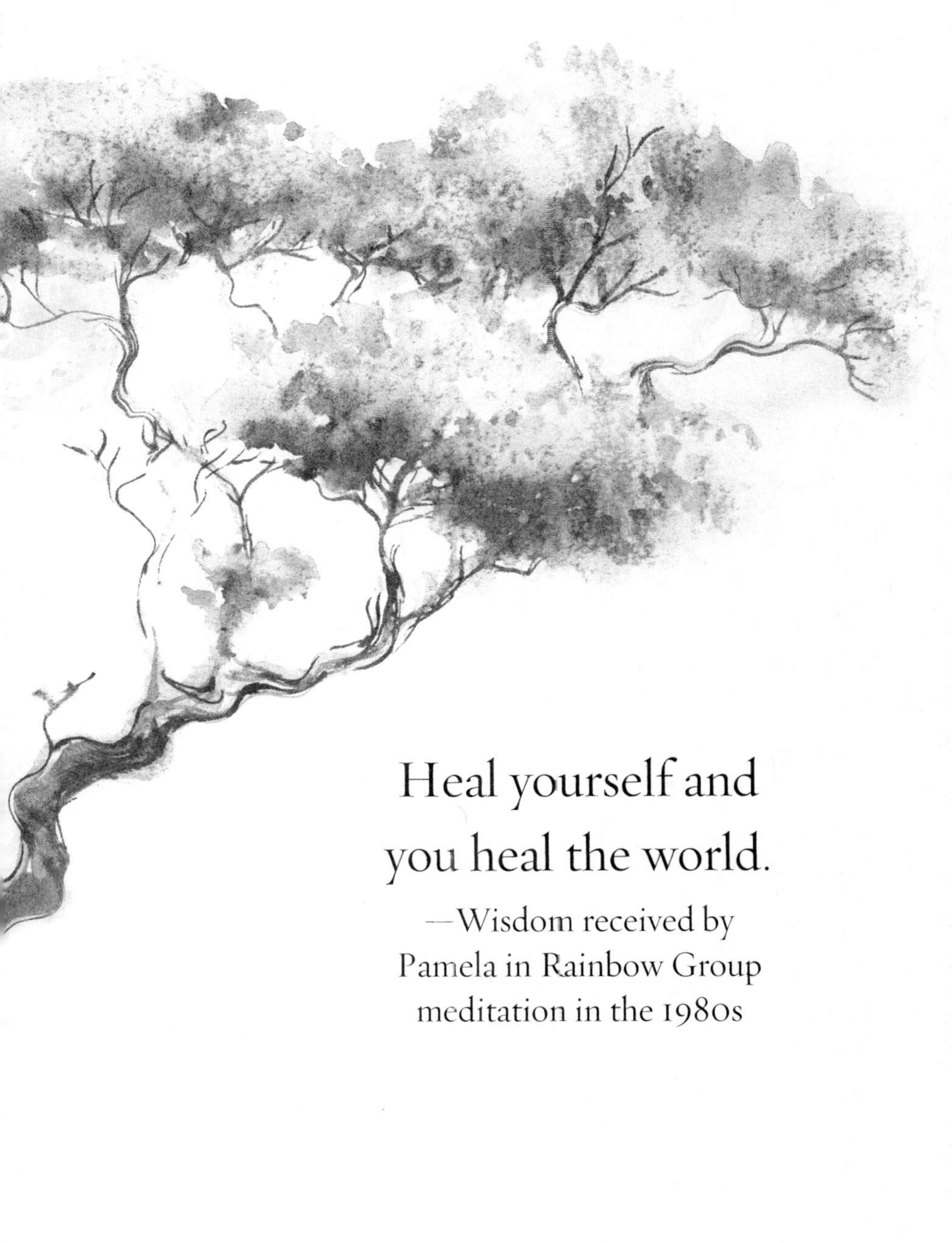

Heal yourself and
you heal the world.

—Wisdom received by
Pamela in Rainbow Group
meditation in the 1980s

The Presence of the Divine in the Mass Exodus of Souls

Patricia

When we were discussing what subject matter to include in *Bringing Death to Life* we were all keen that something be written about man's inhumanity to man down the ages, and about the genocides that have taken place in the past and are still taking place today.

From the time of Genghis Khan to the Roman destruction of Carthage, the slaughter of at least a million Cathars by the Church, the genocides of indigenous peoples, such as the Moriori, Aboriginal and Native American tribes, the crime of genocide has a long and tortured history. The massacre of the Jews in the Holocaust, the genocides in Rwanda, Bosnia and, currently, the atrocities against the Syrian, Kurdish and Rohingya peoples are but a few.

How and why does such horrendous brutality—neighbour turning against neighbour and race against race—take place? It is a question that can seem impossible to answer. When viewed from a spiritual and metaphysical viewpoint, however, some sense can be made of what occurs through the ages in the name of God, religion, political expediency or ideology.

Until we learn that we are all one and come from the same source, the conflicts will continue.

Pam was once given a powerful vision that offers an explanation to this age-old question so she has undertaken to write this ultimately uplifting segment about the darkest of subjects.

Pamela

From an early age, I have been fascinated by the tribes and culture of the First Nations of North America, the country first named Turtle Island by indigenous people. My interest may stem from this: in the early days of Spiritualism, many deceased Native Americans channelled their philosophy through trance mediums in America and Britain. The best known to me was Silver Birch, who channelled his wisdom through Maurice Barbanell, and White Eagle, who channelled through Grace Cooke. The first person my mother channelled, after many years of Spiritual development, was a Native American.

I had always felt sadness and guilt for the genocide of the First Nations of North America at the hands of Europeans. I questioned and judged man's inhumanity to man in the pursuit of material wealth, land and freedom at the expense of the freedom and lives of others. I focused on the terrible things they had done to the indigenous peoples, such as giving them blankets infected with smallpox, introducing them to alcohol and betraying so-called peace settlements.

The colonialists took the best land and gave the worst to the tribes, who were left hopeless and unable to fight for their rights. Their children were rounded up and taken to live in boarding schools, forbidden to see their families or to use their own language, practise their healing medicine, or commune with their ancestors in the Spirit World.

My love for and affinity with the First Nations grew throughout my life, and in 1996 my husband and I went to North and South Dakota where we attended a First Nations "Star" Conference, followed by a pilgrimage to the beautiful Black Hills, the Sylvan Lake and the Crazy Horse Memorial. We climbed the Sacred Mountain, Bear Butte, in silence and walked the Sacred Land where so many lost their lives.

On my return from the visit, I was filled with the beauty and Spirit of the land but still deeply saddened. However, I had also seen a revival of the old ways by the present-day First Nations people. There was a growing movement to return to the values of old, of working with the Mother Spirit and honouring the land.

For many years I was angry about the genocide of indigenous peoples but always hoped we would learn from past mistakes. The genocide of the Jews was an atrocity beyond comprehension.

Although genocide is still happening today, people are increasingly seeing the error of our forefathers' ways. Throughout my life, I have seen the decline of fear-based religions and an increasing awareness of atrocities generated by racism, prejudice and elitism, due to a rise in Spiritual awareness and humanism. For every act of greed, cruelty and violence, billions of kindnesses are motivated by love and shared humanity. The atrocities that play out on the world stage show us that we must always be vigilant in overcoming prejudice, self-interest and inhumanity.

In 2005, after a lifetime of communing with Spirit, directly and indirectly, I started to receive information through meditation that led me to write about the evolution of human consciousness. When words became inadequate I had dreams and experienced visions, which helped me see the bigger picture, beyond prejudice and judgement. I saw life and death, light and shadow, love and hate as a consequence of living and perceiving on a lower frequency, where duality exists. In this state, as individuals and as a collective consciousness, we have lived within a limited perception, filled with insecurity and ego, which sees itself alone and separate, often only accepting others who look like us and are of like minds, believing the same things.

But I, like much of humanity, was beginning to "go within" to what I call "the silent one," which knows and observes only oneness. Many people now have the luxury of time to reflect and meditate. Many are experiencing Spiritual modalities formerly only known by the mystery schools and the elite.

The Western mind was choosing intellectually what the ancients already knew intuitively. We were evolving into wholeness as the two sides of the brain were activated by the software we call Spirit or God or energy or William Blake's "Divine Imagination."

Albert Einstein once remarked that, "The intuitive mind is a sacred gift and the rational mind is a faithful servant. We have created a society that honours the servant and has forgotten the gift." I believe we are ready to make the leap to integrate the gift with the servant into the wholeness of being, bringing the intellect and the heart, the male and female, the yin and yang into balance and alignment.

"The intuitive mind is a sacred gift and the rational mind is a faithful servant. We have created a society that honours the servant and has forgotten the gift."

I would like to share some visions with you that helped me understand the collective journey we are all making from shadow to light, from fear to love, and to the knowing that we are all one light tribe.

Once, when deep in meditation, I was jettisoned through the ether to find myself beside a river holding a baby boy and crying with desolation because my tribe had lost everything—our way of life, our ceremony and our ability to hunt and feed ourselves. We were ruined. We had lost our rich and beautiful culture, built over thousands of years, within just a few months. I cried for my baby, who would never run freely on the plains and grow up in his community in which he would be valued and initiated. He would never know the ways of living with the Spirit of the ancestors, in tune with the Mother and Father God, in honouring the land, and in tune with the animals who sustained us on many levels.

The anger and frustration I felt for our men was overwhelming. I saw them lying on the ground unconscious, empty and without will. They had let everything go, wiped it all out, by succumbing to alcohol.

When I returned to normal consciousness from this experience, I was shocked at my perceptions. It was my own men I had blamed for the demise of our tribe, rather than the white men who for me, centuries later, had seemed totally responsible. That was one shock that led me to experience a different perspective.

Perhaps we need to experience both sides of the coin, as victim and persecutor, to understand what we, as humans, are capable of. We have a great capacity for love, empathy, forgiveness and compassion and are also powerful in creating fear, hatred and evil when love is absent. Only in this universal awareness can we take full responsibility for all the dis-ease in the world and become the healers of ourselves. We can choose in any given moment to return to love or be in fear.

I was led further into understanding the bigger picture when I read *Black Elk Speaks*. John Neihardt met and recorded the experiences and memories of the Holy Man Black Elk, a second cousin to Chief Crazy Horse, whose memorial I had visited in the Black Hills.

Throughout his remarkable life journey—which took him to Europe with Buffalo Bill's Wild West Show, and eventually to meet Queen Victoria, absorbing other cultures and the tenets of Christianity as he went—Black Elk was sowing the seeds for the future unity and oneness of all races, cultures and religions, which he had been shown in visions as a child.

He told of one such vision in *Black Elk Speaks*, where he stood on the "highest mountain of them all" and saw beneath him the whole hoop of the world—and the shape of all things in Spirit. His amazing lifelong Spiritual mission was to share the prophecies of the One Sacred Hoop, the Flowering Tree and the "people yet to be."

He returned to Pine Ridge, South Dakota where he spent his life sharing and integrating the teachings of Christianity he had learned on his travels in Europe with his tribal ways of life. For me, his life symbolised the journey of humanity from the indigenous to the modern consciousness of today.

My awareness was changing: I began to look beyond blame, right and wrong, light and dark in my quest to understand the evolution of consciousness that would further enlighten and prepare the way for the "people yet to be."

It was then I received a vision, which revealed more to me than I could put into words. I was deep in meditation when suddenly I was transported in the ether to Bear Butte, the Sacred Mountain, in South Dakota. Walking down the mountain in silence, I remembered the freedom and exhilaration of a life long ago, running across the plains. Reaching the bottom, I looked upon the beautiful land and upwards to the vast expanse of sky. Suddenly, and out of the blue, they came: a multitude of Spirits from all the tribes. They each had their own dress, embellished with beautiful beads and adornments mainly of red, yellow and black, and they all had expansive rainbow-coloured wings fluttering gently in the breeze as they descended to Earth.

My awareness was changing: I began to look beyond blame, right and wrong, light and dark in my quest to understand the evolution of consciousness that would further enlighten and prepare the way for the "people yet to be."

One by one they came, men, women and finally the babies cocooned in white buffalo skins bringing the new light power to Earth. As the winged infants landed, the red of the soil seeped into the white of their cocoons creating a pink aura of love and compassion that quickly spread to cover the entire land.

These powerful beings grew in an instant to adulthood as the call of the eagle and the raven welcomed them. I looked on in awe as the Rainbow Peoples revelled in delight and danced the dance of ancient times, until slowly a silence descended and came upon the people of all the nations, joined together in one circle. Then, stepping out from the circle, two people from every nation, a man and a woman, each carrying a drum, formed an outer circle surrounding the united tribes. Out of the silence, quietly at first, came one beat, then another and another and another, until all the beats of every nation came together in a harmonic convergence of pure sound, becoming one sacred heartbeat. The rhythm became one with the harmony of the spheres and the world was changed forever in the twinkling of an eye.

All day the beat continued, and went on long into the night.

Moving slowly in resonance with the rhythm of the one heartbeat, I looked up into the blackness of the star-spangled sky where I saw the full moon appear in all her splendour. Then, as if following the moon's directions, every soul on Earth came fully into their higher self. As if in synchronicity with everyone coming into their light, a new star sparked into being in the night sky. Other lights filled the heavens in every direction as far as the eye could see, as beings from other dimensions witnessed the event in celebration and joy.

I watched in amazement and wonder hearing the exquisite reverie of a woman. There, standing on a newly formed crescent moon, a beautiful woman was calling in the tide through a conch shell. Lifting it to her lips, she sang a future dream to all seers who had the star knowledge. This was her song—"The Star Song," which I wrote down.

When the time comes to go
We shall know
When the time comes to know
We shall go
They will come for us in their ships of light
We shall transcend
And ascend in the night.
We'll know it's the time
By the rhythm and rhyme
We'll acknowledge our Spirit Divine.
When the time comes to be
We'll see
When the time comes to see
We'll be

Awakened to who we all are
Seeded blessings
From a distant star
We'll know it's the time
By the rhythm and rhyme
We'll acknowledge our Spirit Divine
When the time comes to go
We'll be led
By Soul Weavers of the
Rainbow web
We'll know it's the time
By the rhythm and rhyme
We'll acknowledge the Spirit Divine.
When the myriads of time have completed
The circle
The worlds will unite on the back
Of the Turtle.

"Why Turtle?" I asked.

The Shell Woman answered: "The ancestors of the Great White Spirit shall lead you to your Divine destiny."

In that moment I was transported back to the carefree child of the First Nations of Light in Turtle Island. Then my mood plummeted as the scene became desolate and I saw millions of my people lying dead, massacred. My eyes were drawn to a group of bloodied bodies where a grandmother sat rocking from side to side, letting out primeval sobs of unbearable loss as she mourned her six beautiful grandchildren, her tribe and the end of their culture.

Almost overwhelmed with grief I let out a cry from the depth of my being, which spread across the mass of sacred bodies. It was as if my cry broke the spell. Stunned, I then saw a Spirit rise from each lifeless body, undamaged and shining with the light of a higher love, bringing a new power that would lead to a new consciousness on Earth. Following their recent death and being between this world and the next, the souls were powerful in their magnetic healing light, which formed a new bridge between Heaven and Earth.

Stunned, I then saw a Spirit rise from each lifeless body, undamaged and shining with the light of a higher love, bringing a new power that would lead to a new consciousness on Earth.

In time people would learn from the mistakes of the past, led by these indigenous souls, who left a blueprint for their future selves to walk again. In many lives, they would experience both sides of the coin but love was in ascendance as the light grew slowly until there was a mass conscious intention to choose to return to the communion with the Spirit and with each other. The head and the heart were finally working together in balance and perfect equilibrium in a new world.

On my return from the vision, I saw that I, too, had contributed to both light and shadow. I hadn't realised that the web of life, contaminated by every thought or act of fear, hatred, aggression and bloodletting, would come together in a collective Zeitgeist of an era when we would all be connected, watch and see collectively the evil rise up to be acknowledged and healed.

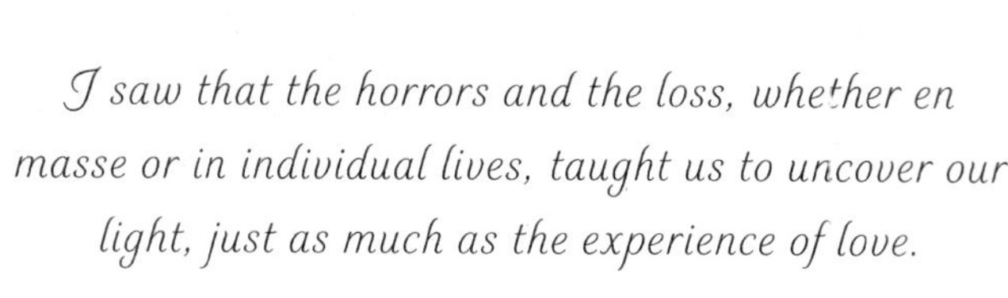
I saw that the horrors and the loss, whether en masse or in individual lives, taught us to uncover our light, just as much as the experience of love.

Now, modern communications technology would make possible the viewing of all atrocities, simultaneously, as they happened, and in time give birth to a time when we would respond, love and forgive rather than react in revenge. We would leave behind an eye for an eye and choosing to be the peace. Evil would no longer be a perception of "us and them." We had to see it in ourselves to heal it. I now saw that the latter was in ascendance.

I saw that the horrors and the loss, whether en masse or in individual lives, taught us to uncover our light, just as much as the experience of love, on this level of understanding. I saw the world being created and destroyed in the relentless march to enlightenment. I saw all the people of old returning again and again, cleansing their bloodline of hatred, hurt and revenge with their soul light until such a time when they would be truly light aware.

I saw the Western mind, now using the left hemisphere of the brain, destroying its own indigenous past in an attempt to take "matter" into its own hands. No longer living only intuitively and in faith with Mother Earth and

Father Sky, the Western mind wanted to possess it, measure it, have total dominance over it, and even replicate the creation of life. It fed upon the material realm with a rapacious appetite in its quest to know and sense everything. Everything was addictive and never wholly satisfying.

The hole has to be filled time and time again until we see the light. But, rest assured, this has been promised, and predicted in many cultures and will undoubtedly happen. It starts with us and, following the Spiritual precept "Heal yourself and you heal the world," it behoves us to look into our own hearts and deal with whatever negative thoughts and resentments we have against others.

When, individually, we come to peace in our own lives, the energy of light will spread, and even though it may be aeons away, by doing our little bit we will contribute to the everlasting peace that is our Divine right.

Mary Helen
A 9/11 Story

Like Pam, I perceive a Divine plan in everything here on Earth, even those aspects of life that are most harrowing, and are beyond the comprehension of our rational minds.

This is one such story where a greater understanding of a catastrophic event became clear to me, in time: the devastation that occurred when two planes flew into the World Trade Center, on Tuesday, 11 September 2001, ending the lives of 2,996 people, and creating untold levels of grief, chaos and uncertainty in America and beyond.

The morning of 9/11, I awoke to a feeling I had experienced numerous times before, which this *Star Wars* analogy best explains: that of the Jedi, feeling a "disturbance in the force" just prior to Darth Vader committing some inhuman act. I dreaded this feeling.

I was alone and such was the sense of foreboding that I didn't want to leave the house. But I had patients to see and so headed in to work, returning to the sanctuary of home at lunchtime, instead of going into town for my usual bite to eat. I prepared a sandwich and sat down in front of the television.

It was one forty-five Irish time when a live news feed interrupted the programme and in shocked tones announced that an aeroplane had just slammed into the World Trade Center in New York City.

I immediately rang my friend Sheila, who hails from NYC, unsure if I was watching fact or fiction unfold, not thinking that I was the first to be telling her that an iconic landmark of her city was on fire, with a burning plane embedded in it, right in front of my eyes.

"Oh, my God! Oh, my God!" she screamed. "What's happening? What the hell is happening?" Just then, the second plane hit.

"I have to ring home!" she cried, and the phone went dead.

I instantly called my parents in America, to be answered by the ever-cheerful voice of my mother, unaware of what was happening. As I explained, she said breathlessly that a close family member who lives in the South was attending a meeting next door to the World Trade Center that morning.

Our family is blessed that our loved one eventually made it to safety. My friend, Sheila, wasn't so lucky. Her cousin, who was also one of her closest friends, was one of the incredibly courageous firemen who lost his life in the catastrophe. In one of the most distressing experiences I've ever had as a clairvoyant, I was able to "see" Bobby, trapped in the rubble and still alive for quite some time before he finally slipped away.

It was weeks before his body was found in the wreckage that became known as Ground Zero. The lives he touched as well as the lives he saved, by sacrificing his own, will never be the same again. This connection to a man that I only knew through his cousin's stories would be relevant in the months to come.

That evening, I sat on the wall between my house and that of Yvonne and Farooq, my neighbours. Farooq sat with me. He was a Muslim from Pakistan who had been living in Ireland for a number of years with his Irish wife. We had celebrated many occasions together as neighbours and friends, and that day, we weren't American or Pakistani, Spiritualist or Muslim, we were two citizens of the world, dumbfounded by the heinous crime that human beings had inflicted on others.

Seeing that attack on human lives from this side of the world put a very different perspective on things for me. I was embarrassed by the number of times over the years that I hadn't given a second thought, other than a quick prayer, to news reports of equally disturbing attacks in other parts of the world.

It doesn't matter where the violence takes place or by whom the terrorism is committed. The extinction of human life, whether by terrorism or "justified" by some government's war, boggles the mind, particularly when it is carried out in any one of the many names of God. That is not, or ever shall be, the will of the God I know. We should remain mindful that just because something is out of sight, it should never be out of mind.

I gained a deeper understanding that day of the contempt in which many other citizens of the world hold America, as our world virtually ground to a halt when we experienced mass tragedy on our own doorstep. How easily we forget the struggles for freedom, the senseless acts of violence resulting in monumental loss of life, which take place on a daily basis around the globe. I'm proud to be American Irish and grateful for the privileges that come with that status. However, I will be the first to put up my hand and admit that I had no concept of what terror really felt like until it happened to my country and to the people I know and love.

A few months later, Sheila and her Irish family organised a memorial service for her cousin Bobby in Kinvara, County Galway. It took place in the church where their grandparents had been baptised and was a classic example of a typical Irish Catholic country church. Sheila had asked me to sing "Amazing Grace" at the service, a request I was honoured to fulfil. During the service, Sheila and I were sitting in the front pew when I gave her a nudge and said, "Can you see that?"

Sensing that something unusual was happening, she couldn't see what I was seeing, but she could feel it. The most incredibly beautiful, glowing light was hovering over the altar and we both knew Bobby was there. I could barely get the words out as I was so overwhelmed by the appearance of the life force, the Spirit of the man for whom I was singing but had never met in physical form. It was one of the most extraordinary visions I have ever had of a Spiritual being, and his presence was felt by all.

Through a lifetime of seeing and communicating with Spirits, I have come to believe—as Pamela has described—that what appears to be tragic within the Earthly realm is always part of a larger, Divinely orchestrated soul plan.

While the souls who crossed in the mass exodus of 9/11 may not consciously have been aware in that moment that their deaths were part of one of the greatest lessons in modern history, I firmly believe that upon return to their natural state of pure energy and light, they became fully aware of the choice to take part in the opportunity to change lives through increased awareness.

We already are that which we seek: Divine, eternal, omnipotent souls who willingly agree to come to this realm not only to grow but to assist in the growth of our fellow souls incarnate.

It is difficult to decipher these things with our limited human brains, chained to five senses and a veiled forgetfulness of who and what we really are. For those of us who have had the great privilege to see beyond the veil, I feel it is our duty to share the insight we've been given that we already are that which we seek: Divine, eternal, omnipotent souls who willingly agree to come to this realm not only to grow but to assist in the growth of our fellow souls incarnate.

Aidan

A Message from the Angels

I've asked my angels and guides a question that is often put to me about the tragedy of genocide: why does God allow genocide to happen? Here is what I was told:

> *The mass exodus of people from their Earthly home, whether it is by genocide, mass murder or natural disaster, is not to bring pain and suffering to the world.*
>
> *God leaves it up to you to reform the world. This is not to say that God has stepped away from us. Remember, He loves you, and will help you when you ask for help. Pain and suffering is always caused by the lack of God in a situation, not because of God.*
>
> *Through mass suffering, we can become more God-conscious, and it is only through becoming more God-conscious that we can end mass suffering. We have seen this happen after many terrible atrocities: the outpouring of help, support and love, which crosses all boundaries of religion, race and political belief. It binds people and brings out the very best in them. But, alas, dear friends, this doesn't always last because politics, old hurts and greed raise their ugly heads again and egos begin to resurface.*
>
> *Again I say to you, God leaves it up to you to reform the world. He loves you, and He will help you when you ask for help.*

Pamela

I would like to end with this inspiration from the Lady of Light, which came following the life-changing events in 22 May 2017, when an act of horrific terrorism in Manchester ended the lives of twenty-two people who were leaving Manchester Arena after a concert by the American singer Ariana Grande.

A Message from the Lady of Light

This is now a peace process.

Let light in.

You have been born here at this special time of awakening and revelation. You are the light of the world, the soul family, and the human race. Many of you are aware of this.

You are pioneers of the work of love and light, preparing the way for the children of a higher light, now returning to this lower realm for the co-creation of a new world. Together you shall engender a great leap in light consciousness. You have stopped fighting the world that was and you are now uncovering the world that is on the brink of manifestation.

You are now a peace process.

You are the light of the world.

You are the embodiment of light. Your DNA is light. You are a magnetic being of love and creativity, emerging from the Great Forgetting.

"Go forth and multiply" refers to light. Light is exponential in its nature.

Each generation has brought a little more light, enlightening the path for your future when, cleansed from ancestral shadows, you can emerge in your true light, radiant and awake. In this altered state of being you shall radiate and awaken those still asleep because, at the root of you, you are all one soul, while experiencing life "in Divine Duality," otherwise known as individuality.

Thus, after many lifetimes, you have created a critical mass of light and power, revealing a higher light visible upon Earth.

For the first time in recorded history you are now connected physically, as well as Spiritually, by your new technologies.

You are now seeing the results of your powerful thoughts and actions, whether they are reactions of fear and separation, or whether they be responses from cleansed thoughts of love and oneness.

You are at your most powerful when you come together in silence, and in sharing the gifts of the Spirit.

Let us meet regularly in uncovering and making more light visible on Earth. Let us always start with tuning in to the silence, where our higher selves reside.

Let us all participate, sharing our awakenings. Let us each share our gifts of Spirit, whether they be in silent radiance, words, dance, song or meditation.

The Holocaust

On the 18th of January, 2018, I stood in the snow-covered courtyard of the Sachsenhausen Concentration Camp, located in Oranienburg, Germany. Exactly 78 years earlier, to the day, over 800 prisoners had been forced to stand in that same courtyard, in sub-zero temperatures, wearing only their "striped-pajamas". On a whim, the Camp Leader had forced the captives to stand at attention for a period of twenty-four hours, something about marking the day that a Jewish man had assaulted an SS officer several years prior. From sheer exposure to the elements, the prisoners began to collapse and die. By morning, 140 had perished.

As I stood there, wearing a heavy, full-length coat and furry hat as the sleet and snow pelted down, I could scarcely imagine what it must have been like as men, women and children felt their fingers and toes freeze first, before succumbing to hypothermia.

The Nazis had called it a "model" camp. One that had been adorned beyond the brick walls, and barbed wire, with beautiful flowerbeds, trees and a park-like setting. Sachsenhausen had been regularly visited by foreign dignitaries and was presented as a political prison where inmates worked in a non-threatening and decent environment.

Beyond Gate A, where machine guns sat, aimed waiting for inmates to cross the line into the neutral zone. Political activists, Jews, homosexuals and those identified by the Nazi party as "anti-social," were being tortured, experimented on and literally worked to death. There were others who were waiting to be hung, shot or gassed.

The prisoners dug clay in nearby pits, and made bricks to be shipped to Berlin, where Hitler was beginning to build "Germania," a Utopian world capitol, free of undesirables.

Those who were considered fit for medical experimentation were subjected to unthinkable exposure to a host of chemicals, as doctors searched for performance-enhancing drugs to assist Hitler in his quest for "super soldiers."

In less than a decade, over 200,000 people passed, or passed through Sachsenhausen. Thousands upon thousands, as in many concentration camps, were heartlessly murdered at the hands of the Nazis.

I heard an English girl ask her boyfriend, "How could God allow this to happen?"

I dare say she isn't the first person to ask this question. As Aidan responds, when the question is put to him, "*Pain and suffering is always caused by the* lack *of God in a situation, not* because *of God.*"

It's hard to get one's head around the idea of such a broad spectrum of individuals being rounded up like cattle to be shipped off to a living hell, all because they were different than "the man in charge."

So often I have been asked during the Q&A section of a speech I have just given, if I actually believe that someone like Hitler didn't go to Hell. In answer to that, one would have to *believe* that there is a Hell, and I, from *my* personal experiences with the after-life, do not. People find it difficult to swallow, that a man who could create such fear and devastation in so many lives, would not be exiled to an eternal damnation to be punished for the great suffering he caused.

I experienced, and now have unquestionable faith in the knowledge, that souls and soul groups are completely aware of they roles that they will play when on Earth. Some have a more personal role within the lives of a few, while others opt to take part in operations that stand to create shifts in consciousness on a global scale.

When an omnipotent and eternal soul decides to take part in a life on Earth, they do so from a place of complete empowerment, knowing that the human condition they will experience is only temporary. There are roles assigned, agreements made, and a being who knows that it is of the Light, and will always return to the Light, is more than willing to sacrifice one of many possible lifetimes on Earth in order to create awareness and change.

The beautiful souls who perished at Sachsenhausen, lived, created and loved with family and friends, the same as you and I, until such time that the soul's plan to be part of one of the greatest AWAKENINGS in human history, called them to serve.

The memory to take part was probably remembered by very few, but circumstances would have these folks and not others, in exactly the right place at exactly the right time, for their lives or liberties to be taken away. Some would survive to tell the tale, others, as one SS officer put it, "would only get out, up the chimney in smoke."

Humans tend to be slow when it comes to personal growth unless the lesson is so large, so in their face that they can't help but sit up and take notice. This is why Mass Exodus continues to this day.

How many of us have heard of a town or village in some far away land being flattened by the dropping of horrific bombs that are intended to kill and maim in the cruellest way. It's so far away, we don't know the people, so we shake our heads, turn to the next page of the newspaper, or simply scroll down on our phones to the next story.

We, the human race, have become so disconnected from one another that souls still deem it necessary to come in and exit *en mass* in order to catch our attention. When souls agree to take part, it is with the *complete understanding* that they will immediately return "from whence they came," having sacrificed a single life in order to bring the opportunity for growth, with a chance to change, to the millions left to bear witness to their unthinkable departures.

For those who took up the mantle, agreeing to return to Earth's dense vibration, the veil of forgetfulness is engaged upon arrival to the planet, and they are able to partake in life, gather tools of human experience, have traumas, dramas and love in their lives until such time that they embark upon the purpose of their mission.

Completely engrossed in the stories of their lives, these souls would suffer the horrors of their final days, before returning to the Light where the pain and hardships of their contributions to the evolution of man's consciousness, would be washed away. What a tremendous gift these souls are to all of mankind.

Today, in the world of instant communication, we can no longer fall back on the excuses, or tendencies to believe, that unless it is happening to our families, our loved ones on our own doorsteps, it doesn't concern us. The world is now on our doorstep, with every newspaper, live broadcast, and post on social media. The Mass Exodus scenario has served to bring us closer to the idea that "we are our brother's keeper," no matter what the location.

Activists have mobilized. Organizations have been put in place to help feed the starving. Medical personnel volunteer their time and knowledge. Sponsorship programs to save dying animal species, are forever advertising for help. We don't have it right, just yet, but every single day, someone new joins a global cause because their conscience will no longer allow them to sit idly by.

Change starts in your own back yard. Engaging in difficult conversations, volunteering your time, donating your money and taking part in the political processes, that eventually play out on the world stage, will move us one step closer to removing the need for large groups to exit, such as those at Sachsenhausen, and countless other examples of mass soul departure. Until such time that we have evolved past this as One World, I extend my deepest gratitude to the bright souls who donate a lifetime, to create the horror, and to those loving souls who endure it, on behalf of those whose silence still makes it a necessary lesson.

Aidan

Like Pam and Mary Helen, I'm often asked, especially when an atrocity has been committed, about why 'God' allows this to happen.

I've asked my Angels and Guides what is the reason that such appalling acts occur and this is what I was told.

> *The mass exodus of people from their earthly home whether it is by genocide, mass murder or natural disasters are not to bring pain and suffering to the world. These souls have agreed on a soul level to leave the earth in a mass exodus to draw unified awareness to a situation so it can be addressed on a global level. They have agreed to this before they were born and their intension is to bring people here on earth to a new level of awareness, understanding and love. These crossings occur to help people to become more God conscious to bring them together and allow their true light of love and understanding to shine in helping and supporting each other in the true sense of friendship. We have seen this happen after many terrible atrocities: the outpouring of help, support and love, which crosses all boundaries of religious, race and political belief. It binds people and brings out the very best in them. But alas, dear friends, this doesn't always last because politics, old hurts and greed raise their ugly heads again and egos begin to resurface." Again I say to you, God leaves it up to you to reform the world. This is not to say that God has stepped away from us, remember he loves you, and will help you when you ask for help. Pain and suffering is always caused by the* lack *of God in a situation, not* because *of God."*

The following words were channelled by the famous theosophist and Manchester-born Alice Bailey in her prayer "The Great Invocation" in 1945: "Let light, let love, let power restore the plan on Earth."

Affirmation for Healing Myself to Heal the World

Let Light, Let Love, Let Power
restore the plan on Earth.

"If having a soul means being able to feel love and loyalty and gratitude, then animals are better off than a lot of humans."

—James Herriot

Human's Best Friend

Reflection on the Death of a Pet

Patricia

Every Native American tribe has a group of Spirit animals to guide it and an unquenchable faith in Animism, the religious belief that objects, places and creatures all possess a distinct Spiritual essence.

Anyone who has experienced the unconditional love that a pet gives them has surely been blessed to have such a gift in their life, as I was with my two gorgeous little cats. I grieved their deaths and miss them every day, but I've been hugely comforted by Aidan, Mary Helen and Pam, who see my darlings in Spirit.

I was very blessed also that Mary Helen, out of the blue, rang me to say she was in Dublin, just as my twenty-year-old cat, Miss Joy, collapsed in my back garden. What were the odds on that? A bestie there when I needed her most.

I will never forget her kindness as she drove Joy and me to the vet, and how she was with me every step of the way as I said goodbye to my precious pet and held her until her eyes dimmed, the living spark went out of them and she passed over in the most peaceful and painless way.

I will never forget either the comfort of the first message from Miss Hope that Aidan passed to me and the synchronicity of the moment he gave it to me, which I write about in my segment.

For all of you who have lost a much-loved pet, and wonder if you will ever see them again, rest assured: they will be there to greet you when you cross over and the reunion will be utterly joyful.

Aidan

"Until one has loved an animal, a part of one's soul remains unawakened." —Anatole France

They say that a dog is a man's best friend, but I think any animal we have as a pet is our best friend and part of our family. For some, a pet is even a soul companion.

When we lose a parent, husband, wife, child or someone close to us, people usually sympathise, offer condolence or try to comfort us in some way. We are allowed to grieve, cry and be upset. We are allowed to express and show our emotions.

For many people, losing a pet can be their first experience with death, yet that loss is often ignored or treated lightly by those who have never experienced the love of a pet. Many people won't understand the depth of your grief. Many suggest getting a replacement, as if that will make everything okay. I remember the pain and the deep sense of loss I experienced when my dogs Trixie and Fergie passed over. Each had been my faithful friend and companion for many years and both had helped me through two bouts of depression at the most difficult time of my life. They had sat with me and slept beside me during those dark periods and never left my side.

When I started to get well they were the reason I went for my walks every day. They'd sit at the front door begging me to bring them out. But I knew they were also saying, "Get out of that bed and get some exercise! You'll feel much better for it."

When I had returned to work they would greet me at the door every evening with great excitement, or whenever I came home, even if I was only gone for a short time.

Pets give us unconditional love and support, something we don't always get from our human tribe. The grief I felt when my dogs passed over was so deep I couldn't eat or sleep properly for weeks afterwards. I felt as if someone had ripped out my heart. I felt empty inside. No one really understood why I was so upset about a dog, and I was often told off by colleagues when I tried to talk about them, even just a few weeks after their passing. It took me many months to get over my grief but I never got over losing them. I still love and miss them to this day.

I often feel the Spirit of these two beautiful friends around me. I can hear them walk into my room and feel them lying beside me on my bed at night. I know their Spirits live with me still and protect me while their love surrounds me every day.

When they died, I asked my angel, Hannah, if we meet up with our pets in Heaven, and she told me that of course we do. They have souls and are created by God.

Erica Jong sums it up beautifully: "Dogs come into our lives to teach us about love. They depart to teach us about loss. A new dog never replaces an old dog, it merely expands the heart. If you have loved many dogs your heart is very big."

When I started doing my healing work, pets who had passed on often came into the sessions. As well as giving my clients comfort and delight, it gave me great joy, reinforcing Hannah's assurance to me that I would be reunited with Trixie and Fergie.

I've often given Tricia Reiki healing, and her gorgeous little cat Miss Hope, who died some years ago, is always a very welcome visitor.

Two years ago, Miss Hope's sister, Miss Joy, passed over and, queenly as ever, her Spirit, too, has made her presence felt.

Pets adore the energy of Reiki. My own darling cat Rita will often sit in my Healing Room when I have clients, and soak up the Reiki energy.

Pets come into our life to be loved, to give love and to show us how to love and care for each other.

Erica Jong sums it up beautifully: "Dogs come into our lives to teach us about love. They depart to teach us about loss. A new dog never replaces an old dog, it merely expands the heart. If you have loved many dogs your heart is very big."

Whatever type of pet you had, they are still with you in Spirit and will be there to greet you the moment you cross over the threshold from this life to the next.

Prayer to Saint Francis for Our Pets

Good Saint Francis, you who loved all of God's creatures
To you they were your brothers and sisters
Help us to follow your example
Of treating every living thing with kindness
Saint Francis, Patron Saint of animals
Watch over my pet
And keep my companion safe
Amen.

Patricia

My two little cats, Hope and Joy, came into my life twenty-two years ago, at a time when it seemed I had neither hope nor joy. I was going through a very difficult time, physically (back problems), emotionally (man problems) and Spiritually (wondering why these "adversities" were happening to me).

I was staying at my mobile home in Wicklow and had been having a cup of tea with my sister in hers, which is next to mine. When I came back to mine, I found two kittens curled up on the settee, one jet black, the other black and white. I didn't know what to do I'd never had pets and wasn't mad about cats. I called in the cavalry, my sister, sister-in-law, a plethora of nieces and a nephew. All agreed I had to keep them.

"I'm calling this one Hope," said my eldest niece, who was thirteen at the time, as she cuddled the little black one.

I took the black and white kitten, looked at her and heard myself say, "Well, if that's Hope we'd better call this one Joy." On that beautiful sunny summer morning, two stray kittens, Hope and Joy, entered my life.

And so it went from there, as my nieces adored them over the course of the summer. Three months old and sisters, according to the vet, they had distinct personalities. Miss Joy was a queen. She'd stalk around imperiously and allowed only so much petting. Miss Hope plodded, but she loved being cuddled and would purr like a train at my touch. I fell in love.

When we returned from Wicklow to Dublin, I was terrified they would wander out on to the road, or stray across the field at the end of my back garden, so I kept them in the house for a week. The three of us were mightily relieved the first time I let them out into the back garden. They were great cats, and never strayed, not even when I moved house several years later.

They were good, too. I had a serious talk to them and told them that the rule of the house was: no walking on kitchen counters, tables or mantelpieces. And when the Christmas tree was up, if they so much as went near a bauble they would be barred to the utility room for the duration. They certainly took my lecture to heart as they behaved impeccably, with manners a mother could be proud of.

Soon I couldn't remember my life without them. If I was out for the day the two of them would be perched on the garage roof to greet me when I got home. Late in the evening, I'd stretch out on the sofa and they'd lie on my tummy. Often the three of us would fall asleep and wake ourselves up snoring. We went to Wicklow every summer and they would loll on the deck beside me, purring ecstatically.

In 2008, Hope was bitten by a tomcat. I took her to a vet who was offhand and disinterested. He told me she'd be fine with antibiotics, but after two days I knew she wasn't responding. I visited another vet, who couldn't have been kinder. Hope was put on a drip, and placed on a snug heated blanket in a pod. I stroked her and told her I'd see her the next day, I loved her and to sleep well.

I never slept a wink that night. Early the following morning I got the call to say she had died. I was stunned. I hadn't even considered that this was a possibility.

I still grieve her loss profoundly and wonder could I have done more for her at the end. She was the most loving little cat. She would sit on my knee even when I was trying to write. All Hope wanted was to be cuddled and she was happy. I'd give anything to see her run in to me with her tail high, as it always was.

When I told my shocked Wicklow tribe the news of Miss Hope, we all cried and grieved. We travelled in a convoy of cars to say our last goodbye. She looked very beautiful, as if she were fast asleep, her black coat thick and glossy, her paws curled up under her. They gave us a room to ourselves, and my cavalry, who are with me through thick and thin, stroked her and told her they loved her. The children were so loving and my three-year-old niece made us smile, demanding of my sister Mary, sister-in-law Yvonne and myself, "Why do you have water dripping out of your eyes?"

Their grief was a comfort to me. Miss Hope was a much-loved cat, not just by me but by all the extended family. There was a little café next door so we decided we should have refreshments after the "funeral." It was comforting as everyone discussed what had happened and their own particular memory of Hope. The children were so earnest in trying to comfort me by telling me Hope was with Holy God, although my little niece, in her innocence (or maybe wisdom, understanding at a higher level the process of reincarnation), said she was just "gone on holidays to Heaven and she'll be back soon." I felt it was important for the children to be involved in the process of grieving Hope. For them, it was an introduction to death.

My best memories of Hope are of her running down the garden, her tail as high as a kite, when I rattled her food. Or curled up on my knee purring so contentedly she sounded as if she was going to burst.

Soon after she died, I was driving somewhere with Aidan, when he looked at me and said, "Hope's just given me a message for you."

"Oh, what is it?" I asked eagerly.

"She said not to worry, she's fine, and not to be feeling guilty. It was her time to go. She said when she came into your life you had no hope, and she has left you with Joy. And she said she likes what you've put her in."

What did she mean by that? I wondered, thrilled to have heard from her and loving the message about Joy.

As that thought came into my head my mobile rang. It was the vet's receptionist to tell me that Hope's ashes had arrived and were awaiting collection. I'd chosen a gorgeous wooden cat, curled up asleep, for her urn!

A few weeks later Miss Joy and I went back to Dublin. Our bond grew even closer and she was the most loving companion anyone could wish for. She was with me for twenty years, and I miss her more than I can say. I never told my dad that she had passed, because it would have upset him: he loved hearing about our tiffs, when she would turn her back on me and ignore me, and the way she would scarper when she sensed that a car journey was imminent.

As Aidan says, people who don't understand the bond that can build up between you and a pet may think they can be replaced. But, as all pet lovers know, it's impossible to substitute one for another. Miss Hope and Miss Joy, the most loving and giving pets to me, are irreplaceable.

Mary Helen

About seven years ago, a young man who had been a patient in my practice for most of his life was involved in a fatal road accident. A year after his death, rather than the typical Irish church Mass held to commemorate the dearly departed, his family decided to throw a party to celebrate his life. They invited all of his friends to share good food and music in an atmosphere of festivity. My girls were quite young, so I simply told them that we were going to a really fun party. They had absolutely no idea who or what it was for. Both of my girls have been gifted with abilities outside the normal senses. Jada showed her uncanny ability to communicate with animals from an early age. I would often find her speaking to our cats and dogs, pausing as if listening to a response, then carrying on the conversation. She would regularly tell us if one of the animals didn't feel well or that they liked or disliked a certain food or activity. Animals were always drawn to her.

On this occasion, later that evening, I was chatting to some friends when I looked over and saw Jada sitting in the middle of the driveway. The family dog was on the ground beside her with its head propped on her knee. In typical fashion, Jada was chatting away to it when suddenly she stopped. She gave the dog a hug, then got up and walked over to the mother of the young man who had died. I couldn't hear what was said, but I saw Jada tug at the lady's shirt as she motioned for her to come closer. When she bent down, Jada whispered something in her ear. I saw our hostess put her hand over her mouth in a gesture of surprise, tears filled her eyes and she threw her arms around my daughter. Jada then ran off to play with some of the other kids at the party.

A while later, my friend came up to me and asked if I had told Jada why we were there. I explained what I had said to the girls. She went on to tell me that Jada, who was six then, had whispered into her ear: "Your boy's dog misses him very much."

Still in disbelief, my friend went on to explain that the dog had, in fact, belonged to her son. She said it brought such comfort to her to know that the soul of the animal had been so deeply in tune with her son and was somehow able to communicate its grief to my little girl.

As anyone connected to animals knows, they experience grief too, and one such case concerns my own pet, Sherman, a rescue dog. When Sherman went into heat for the first time, she was still quite young. Our neighbour's much larger dog, also a rescue, answered the call of the wild before any of us could put a stop to it. An unexpected trip to America had caused me to postpone Sherman's trip to the vet to be spayed and, sadly, by the time I got back, her small frame could not hide the fact that she was pregnant.

The vet took one look at her and said the puppies would have to go. Because of the size difference in the dogs, Sherman would have been in great danger if allowed to go full term. I'll never forget having to explain to two very excited little girls what was about to happen. They were devastated, but they weren't the only ones.

Sherman and her brother, Mr Peabody, were completely and utterly grief-stricken when she came home from her surgery. She cried and he would snuggle up to comfort her. For weeks she whined at night. Jada took some of her teddies and put them in the bed with Sherman because she thought it would make her feel she had her puppies around her. Sherman became standoffish; her appetite decreased and she was no longer the affectionate dog she had been.

Time is a great healer, even in the animal kingdom. Sherman eventually began to perk up and interact with our family. There is absolutely no doubt that she deeply grieved the loss of her puppies. She had no way of knowing that her own life was in danger because of the pregnancy. She only knew one day that she was going to be a mother and the next that she was not.

As I stood in the kitchen, staring at that precious dog's little face, I realised that my story on pets and loss would not be complete if I didn't honour the grief our pets feel. We've all heard stories of dogs who would sit in a deceased owner's chair, refusing to move. I've also heard of dogs lying in despair on the grave of a former master. It's not just limited to dogs. My horsy friends have told me that losing a horse is also like losing a best friend. The bond between horse and owner goes deep, each trusting the other with their life.

While cats may be a little more difficult to understand sometimes, anyone who has ever loved and lost a feline friend knows the depth of sadness their death can bring. Tricia always feels that the Mothers were looking after her, the day her lovely, elderly cat Miss Joy had to be put to sleep.

Do the souls of our pets connect with us? You can count on it. Ask anyone who has ever cared for an animal. These pure expressions of love bond from the heart while alive and return to the Divine light, as we do, when their life here is finished.

I can't count the number of times I have seen and felt the presence of Tricia's cat, Miss Joy, when visiting her home, and she is always remembered in conversation. People can leave footprints on our hearts but there's nothing quite like the paw- or hoof-mark of a cherished pet.

Prayer for a Dying Pet

Higher Power
Our beloved pet and companion, [insert name],
Is on his/her final journey.
We will miss him/her dearly.
We thank you for the gift he/she has been to us.
We trust that in your great kindness
You will restore [insert name]
In your heavenly Kingdom
According to your wisdom
Which goes beyond our human understanding.

"All the great religions
of the world inculcate
equality and brotherhood
of mankind and the
virtue of toleration."

—Mahatma Gandhi

Death Has No Religion

An Understanding Across Spiritual Traditions

Mary Helen

In order to understand better where our ideas and beliefs surrounding death have come from, it is useful to consider their roots. It would be impossible to cover them all, but I have selected a few of the world's religions to contrast and compare their ideas on what happens when humans die. I have attempted to be factual in my comparisons, but these are *my* personal musings on the religions and the topic of death.

The title of the chapter says it all, really. Death does not discriminate. It is not racist, it has no religious preference; cultural background or nationality don't matter to it. Death of the physical body comes to everyone, eventually. What happens after that? Some day, every single one of us will know for sure.

Historically, the ancestries of faith organisations are based on what has been passed down through the written and spoken word, and have not been exempt from "man-handling" over the centuries. Spiritually, we'd love to believe that the interpretations of these doctrines are left up to every free-thinking woman, man and child. As the violence in our past and present has clearly shown us, this has rarely been the case. The cumulative effects of the mixture of religion with politics are the number one cause of premature death in recorded history.

That being said, there are many peace-loving religious and non-religious folk who simply adhere to the mantra "live and let live." Any organised group, religious or not, will often grow a faction of radicals. We see it every day on the news. To point the finger at any single religion blatantly denies the historical involvement of a multitude of warriors across the millennia who, representing a number of different religious bodies, committed countless atrocities in one of the many names of a supreme being. What interests me for now is *what* these people believe about what happens when we die and *how* they came to believe it.

Christianity

"Ashes to ashes, dust to dust . . ." Few Christian funerals that I have attended have not included this line. There are books within the Bible, such as Daniel, that describe the dead as those who sleep in the dust of the Earth. In Genesis, we are told that Eve sinned, depriving mankind of the Tree of Life and immortality. In his letter to the Corinthians, Paul speaks of the Earthly tabernacle, or body, being dissolved by death. It is universally supported throughout any version of today's Bible that the common belief in modern Christianity is that the mortal body is finite.

While the Christian Church bases its teachings about Jesus Christ on the New Testament, both the Old and New Testaments comprise the sacred texts of the Christian religion. Throughout the Old Testament, such as in Genesis, where readers are told that death is not the end but a new beginning for believers in God's promises, we see references to the idea that the soul or Spirit lives on following corporal demise. In Luke's Gospel, Jesus tells the dying thief on the cross that he will be with him in Paradise, suggesting that life goes on following the death of the body. Different scholars and churches within the Christian religion have nearly as many interpretations of death based on biblical text as there are followers of Christ.

The Christian religion has traditionally taught that Death is the enemy, who must be conquered. Corinthians is often quoted when a speaker is summing up the underlying premise of death in Christianity: "O Death, where is your victory? O Death, where is your sting? The sting of death is sin, and the power of sin is the law; but thanks be to God, who gives us the victory through our Lord Jesus Christ."

At no point would I even attempt to argue or debate the literal or Spiritual meaning of anyone's chosen sacred scripture but, with at least two billion followers, it is essential to note that Christianity plays a major role in defining the world's perception of death. More than two thousand years after the historical death of Jesus, many practising Christians would scarcely be aware that early Christians believed that the soul *and the body* would ultimately resurrect and live forever in the new Heavens and Earth. As Paul stated in Romans, he eagerly awaited the redemption of his own body.

There is relatively little specific information in the Bible about what actually happens when people die. Believers are told that at the moment of death they will be cleansed from all sin and made perfect, with non-believers separated from God to spend an eternity in the fires of Hell. Of the mechanics of a transformative process between body and soul that takes place upon demise, there is almost no mention.

In AD 325, the Council of Nicaea was established by the Roman Emperor Constantine I to clarify and unify the many different beliefs about the role of the man, Jesus, known to his followers as the Christ. Severe unrest between the earlier followers of Jesus and the pagan community was causing havoc within Constantine's empire.

The permanent declaration of Jesus as immortal and equal to God, the Father, established the base premise of what is known to us today as modern Christianity. With more than three hundred all-male bishops of the early Church in attendance, they were tasked with agreeing among themselves which texts would be placed in the Christian Bible, deciding between those they felt were Divinely inspired and those that were of "questionable" origin.

At this time in history, the divinity of Jesus, therefore the promise of life everlasting, was not yet clearly defined. The council were told to settle the argument once and for all. It is documented that they burned any texts, as was standard at the time, that did not support their new conclusion. Those who had supported the idea that Jesus was a great prophet but was mortal and not the Son of God were sent into exile following the council meeting. This was *a* if not *the* defining moment of modern Christianity. These beliefs about life and what occurs at death are held by at least a quarter of the world's population, and are firmly founded on the conclusions made, and the texts brought forward, by the Council of Nicaea. There have been other monumental gatherings, such as the Second Council of Nicaea in the 700s and the Council of Trent held between 1545 and 1563, but the core tenets of what is known as the Christian faith today were established in 325, by an all-male council of early followers of Jesus, nearly three hundred years after his death, under the authority of Constantine I in what is now modern-day Turkey.

One thing is crystal clear, regardless of personal or clerical interpretation of how the religion was formally organised: Christianity promotes the belief that the soul carries on after death. Time after time, God tells His people—in books throughout the Bible, such as Isaiah, Joshua, Matthew and Revelation—not to fear death. The notion of Christianity's Heaven and Hell provides a destination for the soul beyond death, thus providing us with perfect insight into the core Christian belief that life goes on.

Islam

Different from the less specific references to the death process in Christianity, Islamic tradition gives a detailed account of what happens at the time of death. Based on text from the Qur'an, Allah decrees Islam as the one true religion. It is believed that life in this world is a test and preparation for the afterlife and everyone has one chance to get it right.

During a cab ride in New York City last year, I was fortunate to have an amazing driver who happened to be of the Islamic faith. He was eager to share and kindly answered a few questions I had about *his* interpretations of what happens when a Muslim dies. He gave me a brief synopsis of his religion's text regarding death. He told me of Azrael, the Angel of Death, who comes at the exact time of passing. Once a body is buried, regardless of how it has died, the angels Munkar and Nakir will question the dead.

Believers who are righteous and have strictly adhered to the teachings of the Islamic faith will have great peace and comfort if they answer the questions correctly. Those who do not will be punished. My cabbie vividly described a most painful "extraction" of the soul from the physical body for those who do not believe or have not strictly upheld the guidelines of the faith. His intonation and gestures made what he said one of the most enjoyable sermons I've ever heard.

The Qur'an clearly states, "Every soul shall taste death, and only on the Day of Judgment will you be paid your full recompense." As found in Christianity, death is not to be feared by believers in the Islamic teachings. Once again, we see an unmistakable conviction that the soul lives beyond physical death.

My cab driver made an interesting point. He explained that as an immigrant from the Middle East, his choice to live in America had caused him to rethink some aspects of his faith. He said that he felt it was not practical for him to observe certain traditions he described as antiquated, within a culture so different from his own. His core beliefs about life and death had remained the same, but he had softened his views on other traditional aspects of Islam to gain from the experience of living abroad. He acknowledged that this was not the way of a true Muslim.

From our entertaining conversation I had rock-solid confirmation that those of the Islamic faith believe in the continuation of life after the death of the body. With many Muslim friends, I was already aware of this belief, but my cab driver's approach to explaining the death process was the most accessible I had ever heard.

The older I get, the more I have come to realise that out of habit, or family tradition, people will declare themselves of a certain faith but, if truth be told, they have picked some aspects of the religion to adhere to and dropped others because they no longer work for them. It's buffet-style religion yet many people aren't comfortable enough to detach themselves altogether from allegiance to the faith in which they were raised, even though they no longer follow its guidelines and doctrines. To each his own, I say.

Hinduism

With a foundation built on the concept of reincarnation, where the *atman* or soul of an individual moves into a new body and life experience, Hindus believe that the physical body is ever-changing while the soul is permanent and without change. *Moksha*, or the end of the reincarnation cycle, precedes *Brahman*, where the soul is finally absorbed into the ultimate reality and the Divine force.

Hinduism is often referred to as the oldest religion in the world, with references of this way of life dating back to 500 BCE. The Vedas, the Upanishads, the *Bhagavad Gita* and the Agamas are the major texts outlining Hindu philosophies and Spiritual concepts.

Again, we find in the world's third largest religion the idea that death is just a passage. Hindus see the death of the physical body as a sort of recycling process and opportunity for the *jiva*, the part of the soul that incarnates, to learn and grow through obstacles and challenges to obtain liberation from the illusion of life. The soul is born and reborn in many bodies, so death is never to be feared.

Buddhism

Founded by Siddhartha Gautama, Buddhism is similar to Hinduism in that it believes in reincarnation. However, it does not believe in a permanent "self" or soul. While Hinduism and the other major religions we have discussed thus far all seek a form of ultimate enlightenment, the goal of Buddhism is ultimately to end human suffering. If guidelines for reaching liberation are followed, the Earthly cravings of an "inexpressible self" cease to exist and nirvana is achieved. Unlike the other faiths, where there is a return to a state of perfection, or light, or an eternal damnation of the soul, the closest English equivalent to the word "nirvana" is "snuffed out, extinguished or ceased to exist."

With the desire to become nothing and the goal of eventually losing the desire not to exist, the cycle of death and rebirth is not feared. The focus is far more on the escape from having to live again and again. While different from the religions mentioned thus far in so many respects, the thread remains true that death is but a temporary state of change.

According to many sources on the Internet, at least a billion people describe themselves as non-religious, agnostic or atheist. For those who do not subscribe to the belief that there is a supernatural soul or pathway to enlightenment, paved by the teachings of a prophet or deity, a more scientific approach to death of the body ensues. The "conscious mind" that identifies with the life form it inhabits simply ceases to exist at the exact time of physical death, with the elements composing the body then returning to their natural state of being. The focus of the life is to extract as much from living as possible, with no concern about what happens when we die because the essential characteristics carried throughout life are present only from birth to death.

Within this category are those who willingly admit that they do not know, therefore do not focus on what happens beyond conscious living. The agnostic will often, but not in all cases, promote a life of non-violence and compassion. With no deep belief or feeling of *knowing* about where we come from or where we go beyond death, the non-religious and agnostic tend to live life for the sake of living. For some, death is the end of the line; others are open to the possibility of an outcome beyond their understanding.

Judaism

A fundamental belief of the Jewish faith is *techiyat ha-metim*, or the resurrection of the dead. In the perfect "world to come," a revitalised body will house the soul. With a firm belief that the "self," or the soul, is separate and distinct from the body, a central belief in Judaism is that life should be sustained because it is sacred. The body houses the soul; therefore the body is an integral part of the soul's journey and should be treated with reverence and respect.

While the Torah, the first five books of the Bible, are the foundation and sacred texts of the religion, there is very little reference to the process of death, except that immortality ceased in the Garden of Eden, and there are several mentions of men who used to be someone else: reincarnation was not a foreign concept to early worshippers.

Jewish text does not distinguish who will be resurrected, other than the righteous. The faith continues to wait for a promised Messiah at which time the already deceased will be resurrected and judged. For the righteous, death is not to be feared, and for the unworthy, the ancient Talmud claims that Gehinnom, or Hell, is sixty times hotter than Earthly fire. It is not the act of dying that one should fear but the soul's final destination if the strict laws of the faith are not adhered to during life.

For its glorious eternal resting place with God and its horrifying depiction of eternal punishment of the disbeliever, it is perfectly clear that in Judaism the consciousness of the soul survives bodily demise.

Religious Folk Traditions

There are numerous sub-categories within the traditional Chinese folk religions practised by millions of Asian origin. There are those who believe in a hierarchy of gods, the dramatic influence of the forces of nature (Earth, air, fire and water), cycles of rebirth and a yin and yang concept of the duality of good and evil, feminine and masculine energy and their delicate balance within the framework of life.

While there are literally hundreds of examples of practices and rituals around life and death, there prevails the common theme that consciousness lives on beyond the death of the body.

As found in many Chinese folk religions, one of the primary goals in life in African religious tradition is to become an *ancestor* after death. Funeral rites and rituals show that there is a proper order in which burials must take place to ensure the viability of the soul post-mortem. For those who are not buried in a certain fashion, some believe that the "ghost" of the deceased will be left to wander between the visible and invisible worlds.

The actual death of the body is often dreaded within African folk culture, yet it is also seen as the start of a person's true relationship with all Creation. Much like the yin and yang, or duality of dark and light, within Chinese folk tradition, all respect the necessity of death in the progression of the soul. Also much like the traditional Chinese, respect for nature and the elements prevails throughout African folk-religious practices. We see, yet again, an unwavering belief that life exists before and beyond death of the body.

Spiritism

With a substantial following of at least fourteen million, Spiritism is a broad term used to refer to a Spiritualistic philosophy of life and death. Its very name implies that its followers believe in a soul or spirit that survives outside the human form. Spiritists study the origin, nature and destiny of Spirits and believe in reincarnation of the soul for the purposes of soul growth and advancement of the intellect. It goes without saying, really, that the Spiritist is a firm believer in the death of the body and survival of the soul.

Ethnic and Indigenous Religions

Ethnic or indigenous religions are associated with a particular ethnic group. The Native American religions would be a classic example of an indigenous practice of faith. The different religious practices and deities worshipped are as diverse as the many tribes across the Americas. There are multiple combinations of Polytheism (multiple gods), Monotheism (one god), Henotheism (the worship of one god without discounting the possibility that there may be others) and Animism (where a Spirit possesses all things, such as rivers, trees, rocks, weather and animals) within the numerous Native American practices of faith.

I remember an anthropology professor explaining that Animism predates Paganism. He said that the term "Paganism" hadn't been used until early Christians dubbed the polytheistic Romans "pagans." From the fourth century on, Paganism became a derogatory term used to describe non-Christians.

The professor gave a very clear description of Animism, within the indigenous tribes of America, as a fundamental thread that united all indigenous people regardless of the worship of different deities within the tribes. There was an understanding, a core human belief, that every living thing and everything able to interact with the living possessed a Spirit derived from a greater Spirit. Called by many different names, this principle can be found from the South Pacific Maori and Aboriginal tribes to the Inuit of Alaska and the Dogon people of western Africa.

With most indigenous cultures sharing the common bond of Animism, it is safe to say that opinions about the animation of the body are deeply rooted in the belief that the soul survives corporeal death. It may return again as another person, it may guide from beyond as an ancestor, or it may reappear as a great eagle or a butterfly. Regardless of what shape or form the soul takes on, indigenous cultures believe that it survives and moves on.

As we have seen from the examples above, it's fairly safe to assume that the vast majority of the planet's population are in agreement that death of the body is a natural process that none of us will escape. What happens after that?

Opinions are as endless as the stars in a clear night sky. There are those like Pam and myself, who have had what are described as near-death encounters, where the soul temporarily leaves the body yet somehow remains tied to it.

Personal experiences with death tend to profoundly change those who have them and quite often magnify or supersede religious persuasion.

I can speak for no one but myself. When crushed at 75 m.p.h. and knocked into the next level of the game of life, I experienced absolutely nothing I had been taught in Sunday school as a child. It was better, more magnificent, and all-inclusive.

"Why separate your Spiritual life and your practical life? To an integral being, there is no such distinction."

—Laozi

The Legalities and Practicalities Surrounding Death

Aidan

As the old saying goes in Ireland, "Where there's a will there's a family row." How many times have we read about family inheritance battles? I am sure most of you will know of someone in this situation or someone who has been through such a nightmare with siblings over inheritance. Families are torn apart and at war with each other over who got what, and who thinks they are entitled to more because they did X,Y and Z. And when the battle is over, what are they left with? A pocketful of money and a broken family.

What I see and hear from clients who have experienced this kind of falling-out is that often there is no way back to a happy family life. The bond is broken, rarely to be repaired. The family is never the same again.

So it was with a client and friend, Jane, who had lived with her parents, caring for them until the end of their lives. Six months after her father's death her mother died suddenly, and the family soon discovered that she had died intestate. Jane had assumed, as had her siblings, that the house would be left to her, as she had sacrificed years of her working life to taking care of her parents and did not have a source of income. However, when this turned out not to be so, her siblings demanded that the house be sold so they could have their share of the proceeds.

From 2006 to the present, the matter has been the subject of many threatening solicitors' letters, and Jane's life has been made a misery, not only because of the legalities but also because her brothers and sisters have turned against her in a bid to get what they believe to be their rightful share. "Eaten bread is soon forgotten': Jane is deeply hurt that they have never acknowledged their debt to her for freeing them up to live their own lives, while she cared for their parents. A single woman in her late fifties, at the time of the financial crisis a mortgage was out of the question.

When Jane got to court, the matter was settled on the steps outside because her solicitor advised her not to go into the courtroom: the judge might decide there and then that the house must be put up for sale. She should settle for the five-year stay the family had offered her.

This had an enormous impact on her life, eventually forcing her out of the city where she had lived all her life to find accommodation she could afford.

Jane says to anyone who might find themselves in her situation:

- Talk to your parents about it, no matter how upsetting or difficult it may be.

- Find out from them what is your situation regarding the family home when they die.

- Once the matter is sorted, and hopefully your parents make or update a will, call a meeting of your siblings and parents, and lay the facts before them, to let everyone know the situation regarding the family home.

Bernadette Parte, solicitor and notary public, has kindly set out for us information about the making of a will and the requirements of probate.

Irish law governs the information in this section, and although there are some generalities, it is important to check the precise laws for your own jurisdiction.

Why Make a Will?

Recent research indicates that people's single greatest fear concerning dying is that their loved ones will not be provided for, yet 70 per cent of us have not made a will (including 47 per cent of parents). The simplest way to ensure that your loved ones are looked after is by making a will, setting out what you would like them to receive. In making a will you choose who receives your assets on death. If you don't make a will, the rules on intestacy apply as set out in the Succession Act, 1965. If the deceased left a spouse/civil partner and no children: spouse, or partner, is entitled to the whole estate. If there are children, the spouse, or partner, takes two thirds and the remaining third goes to the children. Note that if one of your children has died, their share would pass to their children, if there are any.

If there are children only, the whole estate is divided equally between them. Grandchildren would have a deceased parent's share divided between them. If only parents survive the deceased, they receive the whole estate equally between them; if one parent is still alive, they are awarded the whole estate; and so on.

If no will has been made, the deceased is said to have died intestate. The above shows how the estate is divided as a consequence.

While it may seem broadly how you would like to distribute your estate, intestacy can have unforeseen and unwanted consequences: it makes no allowance for gifts you would have liked to make to close friends or charities. It may also mean that properties, where loved ones live, must be sold so that all of the beneficiaries can gain access to their share of the estate.

Think of Jane, whose situation I outlined above—it is not an uncommon one: an adult child lived with her parents, caring for them, with neither an income nor another home. Her surviving parent had made no will, and she had siblings: the house would eventually have to be sold so that all her siblings could have their share in the parents' estate. A surviving parent may assume that their other children would allow the sibling who lived in the family home to remain there but, sadly, this is often not the case.

- In your will, you can name the people you would like to handle the administration of your estate. They are called "executors." They also have rightful custody of the body and will often look after your funeral arrangements and ensure that your wishes are met. If you don't make a will, someone in the family has to take on this role. That person may not have the necessary acumen and organisational skills required for the task. The administration of the estate may be delayed—which may have tax consequences—while it is decided who will take on this role.

- If you have children who are minors, it is essential that you make a will to provide for their needs and to name guardians and trustees for them. If one parent dies, the other remains in that role, but if both parents die, and you have not specified who you would like to raise your children, a court may decide and the agreement reached may not be one you would be happy with.

- If you are a cohabitant—one of two people who are living together in an intimate and committed relationship, who are not related and not married—it is critical that you make a will to provide for your loved one. If you are in a cohabiting relationship and you die intestate, your partner has no automatic right to any share of the estate, no matter how long you have been together, apart from what was held jointly. Many people are not aware of this, so it is very important to know your rights in this situation.

- If you do not make a will, your surviving cohabitant must apply to the courts for a share in your estate, and prove their entitlement to it. At what is already an unhappy time, this is stressful, and completely avoidable by making a will.

- Probate Office fees are doubled if the deceased left no will.

- Making a will is also a tax-planning exercise. Careful drafting and professional advice can result in substantial savings of inheritance tax so it is well worth your while to consult a solicitor or tax adviser to assist you with this.

- Last but by no means least, you will feel great when it's done. Making your will is one of the most loving things you will ever do. You have taken time to consider your loved ones when you are no longer around; you have named your executors, possibly given directions about how you would like your funeral to be conducted, and taken the guesswork out of how you would like your estate to be distributed. Bereavement is difficult enough without our making it more difficult for those we love most. Make your will!

I hope you are persuaded of the wisdom of making a will, and for those of you who have already done so, it's a good idea to review your will to ensure that it still reflects your current circumstances and wishes.

It may also be worth considering making an Enduring Power of Attorney so that you have some control over who will make decisions for you in the event that you lose your mental capacity. Your solicitor will advise you on this.

It is also important to look into probate—the legal granting of the right for the executor/administrator of the estate to distribute it.

Patricia

The Importance of a Living Will

As Aidan outlines, it's imperative to make a will. But it is also important to make a living will too, so that our wishes in regard to our medical care are observed.

I have a DNR (do not resuscitate) stipulation in my living will.

This is of the *utmost* importance. I've heard of many family rows when a decision has to be made about whether or not to resuscitate a loved one, if they haven't made their wishes known. It is always good to have at least two people at the DNR conversation so that there are no misunderstandings when the time comes.

I have chosen the type of funeral service I want, and the hymns I want sung, followed by cremation, and stated where I want the "scattering" of my ashes to take place.

It's empowering to be in control, as much as you can, of your requirements pre- and post-death, and extremely helpful to your family and executors. Don't put it off. As it says in the Bible, we know neither the day nor the hour.

In terms of your will, make it as simple as possible.

And consider doing probate for yourself. It is possible and can save quite an amount of money. Aidan, my sister and I, who were executors for our parents' estates, did it ourselves. The most time-consuming aspect is gathering together the documents needed, and even if you have a solicitor this will still fall to you. The Probate Office couldn't have been more helpful, and we had a similar experience with revenue—indeed, anyone we contacted in the post office, the banks and at the auctioneer's assisted in every way possible. And because we double-checked everything to be absolutely sure, everything went smoothly on the day we had our appointment with the probate officer.

In Mary Helen's segment, she tells us of the practical method her mother has devised to leave her valuables to those she wants to have them so that there will be no confusion regarding her wishes. My father left his instructions in writing, an excellent way of reminding the executors of who gets what when the time comes. As if to confirm what I've been saying in this chapter, my nephew, who had been away at sea for months, came to visit recently. He walked into my family room and glanced to his right at the large painting of a street in Kuala Lumpur that hangs on the wall. "I always liked that picture," he remarked. I laughed to myself. Just a few nights before, as I'd lain in bed, I'd wondered would anyone be interested in that painting: it's rather large. Well, did Spirit guide me or not? I'm *delighted* to know that my painting will have a good home and be appreciated when I go on my merry way to the next life.

Mary Helen

Softening the Blow: When Loved Ones Assist with the Practicalities of Their Passing

Mom is eighty-nine now, thankfully with minimal health concerns, which I put down to her incredibly positive attitude towards life. She had decided to catalogue her belongings in a notebook, then use a "dot system" so that her wishes are carried out after she dies. There are four children in my family. My eldest brother and his wife have two children, my sister has one child, my other brother and his wife have two children and I have two children. Each family has been assigned a colour. Certain family heirlooms have been passed through the generations to the eldest son or daughter; there are paintings, pianos and special pieces of jewellery that Mom wants to go to certain children for her own reasons.

On each of these items a coloured dot signifies the future recipients of Mom and Dad's treasures. There are certain things that each of us has had an eye on over the years. We are all free to discuss our desires with Mom and among ourselves. Then, when agreement is reached, the item is marked with the corresponding coloured dot. Each dot has been recorded in the notebook that will accompany Mom's will: if a dot were to fall off or if someone decides later that a certain item should have gone to them, we will know what Mom wanted. It's brave, thoughtful and a great way for her to ensure that her wishes are met while minimising the risk of future arguments.

Grandchildren fall under the colour of their parents so there is no confusion, leaving the parents responsible for deciding what their children will receive. Each time I go home, I try to help Mom sort through another closet or set of drawers to avoid what I call the Grandmother Clark Disaster.

I am not being dramatic when I say that emptying the contents of my grandmother's rather large home in Winchester, Kentucky, was nothing short of traumatic. Apart from the church organs, grand pianos and remnants of her years as a piano teacher and concert pianist, my grandfather, who had been dead for a quarter of a century, had been a medical doctor. All of his office equipment, including boxes of mouldy old medications, was stored in the creepy basement, along with Grandmother's old freezer. I can still taste the freezer-burned ice cream she used to feed us as children.

My grandmother was an authoritative, highly intellectual and very talented woman. Organisation and tidiness were not among her strengths. I remember coming out of that basement with a bandanna tied over my mouth, trying not to breathe in the mould spores or some airborne residual of twenty-five-year-old antibiotics. I looked at my mother, who was doubled over laughing at the state of me, and told her I'd never let her Spirit rest if she did that to me! I reminded her that I am, in fact, her child who can speak to the dead, so I vowed to plague her for all eternity if she left her house in a mess. We've joked about it often, and she attaches no morbidity to the task of making things a little easier for us when she eventually passes.

If you still have living parents, here's an easy preparation tip: don't be afraid to talk to your folks about their wishes. If they aren't comfortable, they'll make that clear soon enough. You may be surprised by how relieved they are to know that you're interested in helping them to sort through the things that meant something special to them during their lifetime. It's a great way to open up a healthy dialogue and discover fascinating facts about your family.

I rang my mother when I finished writing this section because I knew she would enjoy hearing the part about her mother's house. Mom has an infectious laugh and she was tickled when I recited my piece about Grandmother Clark's mouldy basement. In her finest Southern accent, Mom said, "Oh, my heavens, I haven't done any dots since before Christmas. Well, there's my job for the New Year!"

Start thinking about who you'd like to inherit your cherished possessions, and get working on it. It's one of the nicer things to do when preparing for your walk on the wild side!

Directions for a Funeral

On the night I arrived at my family home in Virginia, following my father's passing, my mother called me into her bedroom. There were a few sheets of paper from a yellow legal pad sitting on the bed. I knew it was something from my father. He loved to write on yellow legal pads.

In his very distinct cursive, there was a paragraph concerning people he wanted to participate in his funeral. His dear Scottish friend, Jim, was to read the Twenty-third Psalm in the brogue Dad loved so much. He also wanted his Thursday-morning men's prayer group to sing a few songs, and for his four children to speak if they felt compelled to do so.

Mom looked at me and smiled. My heart began to race because I knew what was coming next. "If you feel like you can, I want you to do this."

I could think of nothing I'd rather do. I took one of Dad's yellow legal pads and sat in his chair at the kitchen table; the same place he had written more than forty years' worth of history lessons, football games, letters of recommendation for his students and friends, acceptance speeches, motivational talks, Sunday sermons and, of course, beautiful eulogies. I truly wanted to do him proud.

That night, I penned the story you are about to read, which I told as part of Dad's eulogy, which I also share in part below. I invite everyone to take comfort in what Dad made clear to me: it is not possible to mess up either life, or death.

An Excerpt from Dad's Eulogy

In the difficult weeks and months leading up to my dad's passing, we watched as Alzheimer's took a grip on this once sharp, lively and highly intelligent man, and living became more and more of a challenge. In his eulogy, I captured some of this journey and here I'll share the part describing a happening towards the end of his life, when a connection to Spirit brought a beautiful clarity to his mind, on a subject he had struggled with all this life: the concept of punishment in the afterlife. With this moment of clarity came a gift for those of us who witnessed it: the reassurance of knowing that we can't mess up this life on Earth.

> One night, Mom and I had stayed late with Dad. The evening had been very difficult for him and he was exceptionally agitated. He refused to lie down on the bed because he feared he would die if he did. He had told us this himself when he was still able to speak. He was restless, shuffling to the bathroom, to the hallway, to his chair, back to the bed, over and over, as if he was stuck on repeat. Confused and very upset, he went to the bathroom and washed his hands . . . again. It was late. Mom and I were both tired, but her sweet little face never once lost its look of compassion.
>
> Without warning, Dad made his way to the bed. He crawled in under the blankets and was starting to giggle, nearly giddy with delight. Mom and I looked at each other, as Dad lay down and lifted his hand towards the ceiling. He was beaming as he looked up in near disbelief at something neither Mom nor I could see. He spoke, for the first time in ages, with a clarity that caught us by complete surprise.
>
> "Oh, it's beautiful! I can see it. I can see it!"

"What is it, Dad? What can you see?"

He laughed and all of a sudden it was as if I had my father back again.

"It's more beautiful than anything you've ever written about."

He patted me on the hand and smiled lovingly.

"Tell me about it, Daddy. What are you seeing?"

"The land beyond the river, darling. Oh, it's so beautiful."

Mom looked at me as if to say, "Is this it?" I shook my head.

The auric or energy field around dying humans lights up, like fireworks light a clear night sky. Dad's field was weak but still pulsating and there were no sparks flying. I had been present for enough passings in my line of work to know.

"Do you see anybody you know, Daddy?"

He chuckled again.

"Momma! I see Momma and she looks so young!" He reached out as if he could nearly touch her.

With that, my dad's eyes became as big as saucers, the deer-in-headlights look. He gasped.

"Daddy! Oh, my gosh, Daddy is there!"

By now, my mother's eyes were as big as his.

For Dad, this was a very big deal. I never knew my father's father. And I'm sure he was a decent man. According to my aunties, he was a most wonderful person. But for Dick Hensley and his perception of what it took to get to Heaven, his father had not "cut the mustard" when it came to exemplary living. Let's just put it this way: the last person that my dad, diehard in his commitment to his Christian faith and personal discipline, expected to see in "the land beyond the river' was his own father. Dad's eyes welled up and he was overwhelmed with emotion. After eighty-four years of preaching, teaching and believing with all of his heart that Heaven was reserved for those who had met certain criteria, he ecstatically proclaimed: "I've had it wrong, Helen! I've had it wrong all along! Everybody is welcome here." He simply couldn't contain his enthusiasm.

He looked at my mother then at me, half laughing, partly crying, and spoke the most profound words I have ever heard about life to this day.

"You can't mess this thing up!"

My mom looked at me, in the throes of a most sanctified, precious moment, her pale green eyes brimming with tears, and whispered, "Write that down!"

"He plants trees to benefit another generation."

—Caecilius Statius

Healing the Family Tree

One Family's Story

Mary Helen

If I have learned one thing over the years, it's that if someone wants to communicate with me, time, distance or death is no obstacle. And so it was in this following story, concerning close family friends of mine from Virginia, when messages from beyond the grave brought a greater understanding of death—and life—to a wider family.

In May 2007, Gene Touchstone began to get a metallic taste in his mouth. Despite feeling dizzy, this avid golfer went to play a few rounds before returning home dishevelled and disoriented. The following day, an emergency spinal tap revealed acute viral encephalitis and meningitis. This well-respected local pharmacist was now at the receiving end of massive doses of medication, affecting his organs, causing acute renal failure.

The once vibrant husband, proud father of two and grandfather of four had been moved to the University of

Virginia Hospital, where he was fighting for his life. When his doctor asked to speak with the family in the waiting room, not only did Gene's immediate family come forward but his friends from college and his hometown all gathered around. His wife, Debbie, was overwhelmed by this act of love and support.

Gene's body would eventually recover, after he had spent weeks strapped into a wheelchair because he couldn't hold himself in a seated position. Debbie taught him how to take a shower again, to feed himself, along with every other small task that the able-bodied take for granted. Spatial and directional amnesia, due to right temporal-lobe damage, made even the smallest effort exceedingly difficult.

During his physical recovery, the family tried all sorts of medications to improve his well-being. But this once calm and rational man was increasingly agitated and irrational. His daughter, Wendy, expressed growing concern that Gene was no longer behaving like the daddy she had once known. His physical recovery had peaked, and in 2009, the Touchstone family watched a slow and painful decline that would eventually leave him in an indefinite state of disrepair and emotional unpredictability.

In mid-February 2010, one of Wendy's children became ill, and she needed her mother's assistance so that she could continue to work. Debbie obliged, trying to convince Gene to make the three-hour trip to Richmond with her. He refused to go, insisting that he would be fine while she was away for a few days. Debbie reluctantly went without him, arranging for a family friend to check in on him during her absence.

On Saturday morning, Gene rang Wendy's house to speak to Debbie, but she was in the shower. She immediately phoned back but got no answer. She tried again. Still no answer. She then placed a call to the friend who was keeping an eye on him, asking that he pop over to the house and check on Gene.

At this point, Debbie had already packed up and started home, with a gnawing feeling that something wasn't right. As she drove, she was listening to Elvis Radio on satellite, when the song "How Great Thou Art" began to play. It was then that she knew in her heart her husband was dead. Gene was found on the floor of his bedroom at around one o'clock. He had died of myocardial infarction. Three days later, his body was laid to rest. It was 23 February.

That date was also my birthday, and I had an unforeseen visitor at my forty-first-birthday party. The spirit who had been embodied as Gene in this lifetime appeared to me in a not-so-subtle glowing light. He was anxious to share the circumstances surrounding his death, knowing that I would eventually pass this important information on to his grieving family.

That date was also my birthday, and I had an unforeseen visitor at my forty-first-birthday party. The spirit who had been embodied as Gene in this lifetime appeared to me in a not-so-subtle glowing light.

Gene had been fully aware on a soul level of the circumstances surrounding his imminent departure. He had known that Debbie simply could not have coped had he passed away without warning when he had first become ill in 2007. There were practical things she needed to be aware of, household affairs that had to be in order, that otherwise would have placed her under a strain from which she might not have recovered. Her learning was in his prolonged death process, not in the chaos that would be created by a sudden departure.

His children would also have time to adapt. Even down to the day of his death, he unravelled a well-orchestrated plan for the family he had loved beyond words. His refusal to go with Debbie to Richmond meant that she would not be the one to find his body.

On a conscious level, Gene told me that he was not aware he was about to die, but on a soul level, he had been completely cognisant of his impending exodus, not leaving out a single detail. By taking the time to turn up on my birthday, his burial day, he was making his final loving gesture to the family he adored. He had not been "the real Gene" for quite some time. On the night of his funeral, the real Gene, the beautiful soul who had played his role so well, came back.

"Get on with it," he playfully asked me to tell his wife, among other detailed and personal revelations. He was eager for her to grasp "the big picture," which he now completely understood in his Spiritual form. He wanted to support Debbie in a different way from how he had in life. His appearance after death would start that ball rolling.

I phoned my mom and told her what had happened. Never surprised, but always intrigued, she acknowledged the enormity of it all. She is always so good about that. I asked her to give Debbie a ring the following day, pass on my condolences and tell her that I would be speaking to her soon. Mom had no intention of telling her why I would be calling, but a five-minute conversation soon turned into an hour.

My dear mother is quite the healer herself. Her gentle nature, her non-judgemental tenderness, all created a safe space for Debbie to open up and share her heartache. The timing was just right, and Mom ended up sharing part of our earlier phone conversation with Debbie.

It would be the following June before I had the opportunity to sit on Debbie's back porch and tell her all. Her daughter Wendy was there, and on that night, Gene made a second appearance. He encouraged his daughter to focus on making some personal changes in her thought process. Life had been tumultuous, and he made it clear, using me as his conduit, that he was completely aware of what had been going on in her world. These were things I could not have known until he literally whispered them in my ear, as Wendy sat right in front of me, validating each comment.

I asked Wendy and Debbie how much they really wanted to know about Gene's passing. They agreed that they needed the entire story, no matter what that meant. What was revealed was the message of a soul plan, leaving no stone unturned, one that created an understanding of life beyond death, one that these two women had never fathomed. He spoke of his beautiful connection with his grandchildren, and that he also knew the day would come when his wife would allow herself the freedom to love again. No one would be like Gene, but why should Debbie experience the same type of love twice in one lifetime? The time would come when she would love as a mature, experienced woman, her family reared, when her time was finally her own. The circumstances would be completely different from the day when a beautiful, inexperienced girl married her dashing young sweetheart and embarked on the challenges of raising a family with him. Debbie would have the chance to learn love in a different form, according to her deceased husband. While new love was the last thing on Debbie's mind, Gene was making it crystal clear that she would, in fact, love again. Can you think of any message more moving?

For me, Debbie was no longer Wendy's mom, as she had been when I was growing up. Gene's death had forged a friendship I now cherish. Wendy and I had been forever friends and shall always remain so. Only now we share something just a bit out of this world. Debbie also gave me a morsel of wisdom that I have used with numerous people who are grieving the slow death of someone they hold dear. She has absolutely no idea how many lives have been touched by this one simple comment. In her infinite growth and understanding of her husband's death, Debbie made this profound statement: "I had to live with my husband damaged in order to let him go."

Following Gene's passing, Debbie spent a tremendous amount of time releasing, letting go and really trying to understand the circumstances around her relationship with her husband. She had to face what I believe is a human being's most difficult challenge ... to sit with one's self. Not easy when you've been with someone for over forty years.

Debbie was in an unusual situation for an individual in her sixties. Both of her parents were still alive. In their nineties, they were still living, unassisted, in their family home in Danville, the next town.

In February 2013, Debbie's mom, Irene, was leaving a church meeting with a friend. She was in the passenger seat when the woman driving the car pulled out in front of a large truck, which struck Irene's side of the vehicle. She broke her arm and wrist and was very shocked, but survived. After her discharge from the hospital, she was moved to a nursing home for rehabilitation.

Just two months later, in April, Debbie's father, Howard, had a series of bad falls, resulting in bruising on the brain after a very serious head injury. He was admitted to the same nursing home as his wife but into a different room. Irene had not wanted to share a room with her husband of over seventy years because she said he talked too much! Howard's recovery was difficult, as he had to be restrained due to the brain injury. Remarkably, both parents healed, and in June they were able to return home under the watch of twenty-four-hour carers.

In July, Irene told Debbie that she had experienced a most vivid dream in which God had told her she would die in two weeks. Debbie had gone to Danville to visit her folks with her sweet little schnauzer, Lexi. Usually, Lexi would make a real fuss of Debbie's parents, snuggling up, looking for affectionate pats on the head. That day, the dog refused to go near Irene.

Later that day, after Debbie had returned to her own home, she received a phone call saying that her mother had suffered a stroke and was being taken to the hospital. By the time she made the half-hour drive back, her mother had sustained a second stroke and Debbie was faced with the decision of whether to have her intubated or to let her slip away on her own. A Do Not Resuscitate, or DNR, was in place, and Debbie struggled when faced with the decision. Her mother was suffering, but Debbie felt very strongly that her father should see the love of his life just one more time. The grandchildren were called and had the opportunity to see their grandmother, but Debbie encouraged all to return home: she needed to sit with her mother's death process in her own way. She had the loving support and nursing expertise of her cousin, Nancy, and I had just arrived from Ireland for the summer.

"The most difficult and the most glorious thing I've ever done." This was Debbie's description of removing her mother's breathing tube.

For anyone who has not experienced the death rattle, it can be terribly distressing as an observer. Human instinct nearly demands that you intervene, help the person to breathe—do something, anything to ease the suffering. For me, Irene's death rattle was an entirely different event.

Before Irene's breathing became laboured, she had begun to demonstrate a feat that I have been fortunate to witness at a number of passings . . . including my own.

There before me, as plain as day, Irene's Spirit, her essence, her energy body, began to rise out of the physical body and hover. It was as if she knew that it wasn't necessary to experience her final hours in the hospital bed, hooked to machines and monitors. Irene's true self simply watched as her body began to wind down and prepare to die.

Irene's favourite hymn was "Jesus Is Tenderly Calling." In the wee hours of the morning, my mother sat at her piano and played into the phone, as Debbie and I sang to

Irene. The wonderful Irish nurse tending her had looked up the words to the song and printed them out for us. She watched with tears in her eyes as the room filled with the glow of the unmistakable presence of the Divine light as we sang Irene through her passing.

Over the next few hours, Irene flat-lined on nine different occasions. I watched her Spirit disappear and reappear from its perch in the top corner of the room. I was fascinated by what took place during this time. When Debbie tried to hold her mother's hand when she was "out of the body," she experienced a terrible electric shock sensation. When she was "in the body," Debbie was able to touch her without consequence.

I tried it myself and twice got a jolt that nearly knocked me off my feet. It was as if Irene was highly charged when out of, yet still tied to, her dying form.

I encouraged Debbie to close her eyes, wrap up in a blanket and snuggle into the armchair for a while. No matter how reverent the process is, the death rattles of a loved one can be unnerving. She rested, and I sat with Irene until the counts between breaths became so prolonged that I told Debbie the time had arrived. With a few final heaves of her fragile chest, Irene finally slipped into the beautiful beyond with her loving daughter by her side.

After the funeral, for which Irene had left detailed instructions, we ruminated on Debbie's back porch about her mother's parting from this world. It had been a beautifully heart-breaking occasion and now she was wondering how her father would handle being on his own. It was then I shared with her that it would be a matter of weeks before her father passed.

A week later, Howard was hospitalised with kidney issues. I went over to the now familiar halls of the Memorial Hospital and set out to assist in making his transition as peaceful as possible, however long it took. I used the Solfeggio tuning forks to clear Howard's chakras. When I flooded his energy field with 528 hertz, he smiled, put one hand on his heart, reached up with the other and, remarkably, turned a corner.

Debbie's prayers were answered when Howard was able to return to his own home, to be the centre of attention or "top dog," as she put it. His life had revolved around Irene, always putting her first, and Debbie was delighted that he would now be the focal point of everyone's affection.

His grandson Steven came home and spent time working on physical therapy with Howard, who rallied for a few weeks.

By now, several years later, just as Gene had prophesied, Debbie had indeed found love again, and was engaged to be married to Ben, an old childhood friend. They were due to go to a wedding in New Orleans, and she was distraught at the idea of leaving her father, but after many late-night discussions on life and death, she understood that her presence might be preventing him from moving on.

The day before Debbie left for New Orleans, my mother and I went over to Danville to visit with her and Howard. The family was blessed to have found the most loving sitters to be with him in his final days. The role of carer is so important and can literally make or break the final precious moments for a family. That afternoon is one I shall never forget.

My mother's last days with my father had been very much as I previously described. My parents had been so close, my father so involved with my mother's life that he had to push her away in his last few weeks of Alzheimer's. One of his carers had been there to witness his passing, not my mother. Paul, the carer, told Mom that he had never known my father as a younger man but he had caught a glimpse of what Dad used to look like just before he passed. Paul described a morphing of sorts, in the wee hours of the morning, as Dad's face became youthful just before the body began to glow and his Spirit lifted out. Never having experienced a death before, when he "saw the light," Paul said that my father's death had changed his life forever.

Now I was standing in Howard's room, only a year after my own father had passed. I called in Debbie, the carer and my mother. I knew in my heart of hearts that they would be able to see what was happening in front of me. The room lit up: tiny lights were popping all around, like a miniature fireworks display. This is a common feature in my numerous experiences over the years of sitting with or assisting someone in their death process. The auric or energy field takes on the appearance of a fireworks display.

For those who can see this energy, the pulsating light, often visible in multiple colours, begins to sparkle and pop as the soul prepares to transition from the body.

For those who can see this energy, the pulsating light, often visible in multiple colours, begins to sparkle and pop as the soul prepares to transition from the body. This is due to the energy field increasing its vibration to escape the dense human form it has resided in throughout the lifespan.

I watched the carer put her hand over her mouth. Debbie and my mother were softly crying and I sat in wonder at the misunderstandings so many have about the miracle of death. My mother, having missed her husband's grand exit, was now privileged to see the beautiful demonstration of a soul's passing from one realm to the next. The carer would never see death in the same way again, and Debbie could let her daddy go, knowing that the Divine process was perfect in every way. It was now only a matter of time ... and Debbie's departure.

In a moment of flawless lucidity, Howard looked at me and asked, "When is she leaving?" He was ready to go home, but he knew that he couldn't take his leave until Debbie was out of reach.

The following day, 30 October, Debbie left for New Orleans. On 1 November, Howard's carer called me to come to the house. I sat in those final moments with Howard and his minister, Jeff. A light began to emanate from Howard's crown chakra. Two luminous beings, distinctly not family, hovered nearby. Jeff, not only the minister but a dear family friend, prayed with Howard, and I sat in deepest gratitude to be so fortunate to witness this most auspicious moment in another human being's story.

I love the healings, the reconnections and the wonderful occasions I have been privileged to observe and participate in over the years, but to be present and to sit with death, the closure of a soul's time here on Earth, for me, is the grandest honour of them all.

When Debbie returned from New Orleans, we talked about what she wanted to do for her father's funeral. She kindly asked me to speak, and it was then that she felt it would be important to share the real events surrounding her father's passing. Howard had been a grocer, a veteran of the Second World War and a pillar of his community. Just two weeks short of his ninety-fifth birthday, few of his closest friends were still living. For those who were, Debbie felt she could best honour her father by telling them what really happened . . . and so I did. The funeral was lovely, traditional for the most part, until I stood in front of the crowd and told them what had transpired on the afternoon when Debbie, my mother, the carer and I had watched the heavens open, preparing Howard for his journey home.

When I was walking out to my car afterwards, two gentlemen, lifelong friends of Howard, approached me. One spoke: "Young lady, I want to thank you. I want to thank you for telling the truth. When you get to be our age, you find yourself going to a lot of funerals. The preachers give some nice sentiments and thoughts about what waits for us, in biblical talk, but this is the first time I've ever been to a service where someone told me what actually happens when you die. At our age, it's literally just around the corner. I can't tell you the comfort and reassurance you gave me today. Thank you for your honesty."

His friend, in a blazer with a Second World War veterans' pin on the lapel, nodded and agreed. Debbie's instincts to share her father's story had been spot on.

The wrap-up of this amazing series of events took place on Debbie's back porch. I'll never forget the wind chimes. When we mentioned her husband's name an unmistakeable tinkle would play out, even if there was no wind; and the butterflies . . . they arrived in quantities not typical for late autumn in the foothills of the Blue Ridge mountains.

"Little Orphan Debbie," as she jokingly referred to herself, had come a very long way in her own understanding of healing since her husband's death in 2009. When he had first become ill, Debbie recalled crawling into the bed next to Gene, begging him not to leave her. Four years later, with her own father, she had learned to respect the space enough to let him go peacefully. With Gene, she was hanging on for dear life; with her parents, she chose to participate proactively in their passing in a way that honoured them, as well as her own growth and understanding. When she realised she couldn't be by her father's side at the end, she was able to step out of the way, gracefully allowing him the space he needed to leave this life behind. Her circumstances with her mother had required her presence and she had made herself available not only physically but emotionally.

Debbie had done so much work on herself, opening up to a new understanding of what it means to heal the family tree. The time I spent with her was deeply meaningful in my life as a facilitator. The sheer privilege, the trust and the honour to watch her evolve has impacted on how I work with others in a most beneficial way. Without her willingness and total honesty, this would not have been possible.

"While I thought
that I was learning
how to live I was
learning how to die."

—Leonardo da Vinci

The Final Act

Making Our Own Preparations

Mary Helen

After pouring so much of myself into the stories I have shared in these pages, it seems appropriate to draw things to a close by sharing some thoughts about my own death, and my preparation for it. I know that Aidan, Pam, Tricia and I can all say, without hesitation, that none of us fear death. I hope we have successfully managed to get that point across throughout this book.

However, our circumstances are very different, in that the practical preparations for my co-authors do not include the care of children. Tricia and Aidan do not have children and Pam's are adults with children of their own now. I am still in that crazy time when the guy at my local petrol station regularly says, "Didn't I just fill you up yesterday?" A single mum, with two teenage girls to look after, I am constantly on the go. If anything were to happen to me, it is my sole responsibility to make sure they are cared for. An insurance policy makes certain that they will always have a home, and that they will be financially secure and educated until adulthood in the event of my death. Although I have it on good authority from my guides and counsel (about whom I wrote in my earlier book *Promised by Heaven*) that this will never be used, my ego is not so big that I would neglect to have this simple solution in place.

This takes me back to childhood when I once saw my mother removing some documents from a strongbox. I was about ten at the time and I was curious to know what the papers were. My folks were preparing to take a trip to Britain and the Republic of Ireland and had just made sure that their wills were in order. Mom tried to explain what a will was. I was perfectly fine until the part where it said that, in the event of their deaths, I would be left in the care of my sister!

I freaked out! My sister is ten years older than me and at that time, when she was a twenty-year-old college student, I was definitely not her first priority and rightly so. I was horrified that my parents could even think of doing that to me. My life would be ruined, and so would hers!

I always felt my sister understandably resented it when my parents regularly left her to babysit me when we were younger, so I could only imagine what it would be like if she was responsible for raising me! As I write this, I think that might have been the moment that sparked my need to know when my parents were going to die. As I said earlier in the book, my grandfather in Spirit answered my question shortly after.

To be honest, I think I've been preparing for death for most of my life. My parents were both history buffs. No family vacation was complete until we had spent time in a cemetery or on some historic battleground. I was accustomed from an early age to strolling through graveyards, reading tombstones and learning the history attached to the time and place in which those souls once dwelled. I saw graveyards as a place of peace and learning rather than as something to fear.

My father was a preacher, so eulogies were always on the go in our house. I suppose what made it easier for me was having my deceased grandfather as my childhood companion. I eventually figured out that *dead* in our world simply meant *no body*, after my parents explained to me that my grandfather, Judge, had been dead since I was a year old. I could still see him and was in constant communication, so "dead" meant something entirely different to me than it did to other people.

I remember being in a graveyard in Old Salem, North Carolina. I was mesmerised by a tombstone that said, "Only sleeping." It was then I decided I would have something funny on mine when I died, like "I told you I didn't feel well," or "Hey! You're blocking my light!" I will admit, although I wasn't afraid of death, I used to think it was creepy when my parents visited their own plot at the graveyard. I get it now, but back then, I thought it was so weird.

The only time I had ever seen the Spirit of someone deceased hanging around the graveyard was if a living person was there, grieving, while the light and love of the departed soul surrounded them. Otherwise, that horror-film depiction of zombies and ghosts creeping around the local cemetery was just *so* Hollywood.

Following my near-death experience in 1991, my preparation for death took on a whole new meaning. The vivid recollection of what it was like to die physically took the mystery and fear out of my own death when it happens the next time around. The greatest tool I have found in my preparation for death is my attitude towards life. I wake up each morning with an indescribable gratitude for the privilege to be alive. I have aches and pains, the lasting effects of a broken neck and twisted spine; I have bills to pay and debts to clear, the results of having taken risks in life; I feel lonely sometimes, the product of having loved and lost with the potential to love again.

Every single morning I ask myself before my head lifts from the pillow if the pain I am in, be it physical or emotional, is bigger than whatever I want to accomplish that day. The answer is inevitably no. To live is not for the faint-hearted and, no matter how tough things have been, if you are reading this now, you have a perfect track record, a one-hundred-per-cent survival rate thus far.

My father once said of life, "We can either embrace a false sense of humility, failing to recognise our gifts as fully as we could, or we can fall into the clutches of pride and arrogance so totally that God no longer uses us in mighty ways, or we can recognise that struggle is inevitable to the human condition. If we bear it courageously, it can teach us an endurance that we can pass on to others in their time of need. There is a joy in this teaching, for it strengthens us in our quest for meaning, which is what makes us human. To remove the struggle is to deny our humanity."

I suppose the most important thing to me in preparation for my own death is to know I am living in such a way that people will remember that something I did, said or wrote made them think more deeply, feel a bit lighter, love more courageously and live a little larger. Of many things in life, I have my opinions, but of one thing I am certain beyond any doubt: death is not the final chapter.

Pamela

The greatest bard, William Shakespeare, speaks to us about life and death: "*Thou know'st 'tis common, all that lives must die, passing through nature to eternity . . . If it be, why seems it so particular with thee?*"

Although common and unavoidable, the experience of life and death is unique for everyone. Death is the final act of life and I'm happy knowing that what I have prepared for my funeral will reflect my values in life, and my family's task will be made easier when the time comes.

My husband Simon and I have taken care of our wills and I would like my funeral arrangements to be carried out by our local undertakers, who are a long-established family business, and who have looked after most of our family. They remember our names and our loved ones.

Simon has done a number of funeral services starting with that for my uncle Fred, who chose him because he was "th'only one int" family who talks proper." Of course, he would be the ideal person to do mine but, talk proper or not, I would hope he might be a bit too emotional for that!

I would love Aidan to take my funeral service, not only because he is a wonderful celebrant but mainly because we have shared so many good times and so much laughter. Like Tricia, I would love there to be laughter at my funeral. There's nothing I like better. But I know there will be tears too.

The final gift to my loved ones will be the songs I have chosen as my epitaph. The first piece represents the miracle of life on this beautiful planet. The second affirms my knowing that at all times during life we are accompanied by angels and Spirit guides, often our loved ones. The third will speak of the beauty where I shall dwell, in so-called death, and where I shall be at my most vibrant and alive.

When the day comes I shall be in the most beautiful place of love and light. My mam will have met me and taken me to be reunited with my loved ones, and I will be at one with the shining beings who have guided me all my life. I shall be embracing many wondrous things.

I shall be sending all my love and gratitude to my lovely family and friends, who have filled my life with love, happiness, the best and saddest of times. I have given them the same, and I know that they will have to go through the process of loss and pain, which is inevitable on this material realm where the pain of loss is a testament to our love.

Eventually they will be aware that love is never extinguished and that Grandma and I shall be watching over them as we did in life. Later down the line I shall be waiting for them with open arms when they, too, make their transition.

Aidan

As I've said throughout this book, I'm not afraid of dying but, like most of us, I'm concerned about the *manner* of my death. This is a very human fear, as we are here to live and experience life with all the joys and pain it brings.

So now, dear reader, our time together is over, and my wish for you is that our book has brought you a greater understanding and peace of mind about the experience we call death. I'd like to share the first stanzas of a poem by Emily Dickinson that most of us know from our schooldays: it gives yet another view of death. The first lines say a lot about her profound knowledge of that which comes to us all, and encompasses all that we have written about in this book.

Because I could not stop for Death –
He kindly stopped for me –
The Carriage held but just Ourselves –
And Immortality.

It's utterly comforting to think of the "kindness" shown by Death, and it has been my experience that Death comes kindly to all, no matter the circumstances of your going, whether it's "sudden," "tragic," "timely," or otherwise.

Many people *do* recognise this, which is lovely to see, and they put on their death notices "Safely home."

For me, that says it all. So when it's time for you to pass, never doubt that you, too, will arrive safely home.

Patricia

When Aidan and I were putting our finishing touches to the book, he gave me a Reiki healing. I was delighted to have one, because if Dad came I wanted to ask him exactly *when* he had left his body at the moment of passing, *who* was there, *what* it was like, and if it was painful at all, so that I could use it in the book if he was happy for me to share it.

Aidan had just done his calling-in, to all our angels, saints, guides and ascended masters, and I felt a lovely energy wash over me. I knew immediately that both my parents were there. Aidan told me that Dad was vibrant and strong again, ready to tell me all I wanted to know, and that he was happy for me to include it in the book. Hadn't he told Mary Helen, using Morse code, one evening that she was staying with me, that he would be helping us?

I asked my questions and he told me that, first, he was absolutely pain-free at the time of his death: all his pain had left him several days previously. That was very comforting to know, as he had stoically endured a great deal, although we had noticed in the two days preceding his death all pain had left his face and a healthy colour had returned, making him look years younger.

He described the moment of death for him as like standing at the starting line of a race, waiting for the starting gun. Then my mother came to him, and he left his body to greet her. Behind her there was a wondrous light and all his loved ones were gathered waiting for him (even my two little cats). It was all a bit overwhelming, he said, adding that, as I'd often told him would happen, he had never looked back.

He said it was *exactly* how I had often explained it to him, and that leaving his Earthly body took no effort at all; he was so glad I was with him as he crossed because I knew about death. He said he now knows that he is in the "resting place" but that the soul's journey is continuous. He said he wouldn't have believed me if I'd told him *that* when he was on Earth, but now he sees the Divine Plan very clearly.

He's very, very happy, and so is my mother. Really, time passes so quickly, he said, although we don't realise it on Earth, and we will all be reunited "in the blink of an eye." And he told me that, as ever, he'll be keeping an eye on the bestseller lists. He used to check them in *The Irish Times* on Saturday, and I loved it when he rang to say proudly, "You're number one again," when I had a new book out.

So, dear readers, how much more reassured could I be that my parents are as near to me now as when they were alive? It is truly comforting, and I hope that you, too, will discover for yourselves that our dearly departed are just a thought away.

My end will be quite simple really. At my funeral there will be no eulogies, plenty of hymns and I'm going to have a letter read out that starts off:

> *My Darlings,*
>
> *I hope you're all howling and that you've brought plenty of tissues ha ha … !*

A good laugh is vital, in my view, because I love a good laugh myself.

I've told my executors there has to be one last "elbows on the table" hooley, to be paid for out of my estate.

Like my three lovely co-writers, I don't fear death, I just hope it's quick and painless.

My last words to you, before we part company, are to remember, as John O'Donohue so memorably put it—changing my view of death from the moment I read it—that our Unknown Companion through life, from the moment we are born, is Death, and we are together on life's great adventure. I hope, through reading this book, you have become more intimate with your own Unknown Companion, and more at ease in its company.

Yes, death will always bring devastating, unbearable grief and sorrow to our lives, and no matter how much we know that we will meet our loved ones again, the loss of them has to be painfully endured.

Aidan, Pam, Mary Helen and I hope that this book will bring some comfort and ease, especially to those of you who are bereaved. We hope that the knowledge we've shared will help shed some light on the *mystery* of death, knowing that it's truly *not* the end, and that, as my dear dad told me, from beyond the veil, "The soul's journey is continuous," and our loved ones are very near.

I think this beautiful, comforting and much-loved poem says all we need to remind ourselves of when our life-long companion makes an appearance through the death of a loved one, or when it's our turn to take Death's hand and be guided home.

Death Is Nothing At All

Henry Scott-Holland

Death is nothing at all.
It does not count.
I have only slipped away into the next room.
Nothing has happened.

Everything remains exactly as it was.
I am I, and you are you,
and the old life that we lived so
fondly together is untouched, unchanged.
Whatever we were to each other, that we are still.

Call me by the old familiar name.
Speak of me in the easy way which you always used.
Put no difference into your tone.
Wear no forced air of solemnity or sorrow.

Laugh as we always laughed at the
little jokes that we enjoyed together.
Play, smile, think of me, pray for me.
Let my name be ever the household word that it always was.
Let it be spoken without an effort,
without the ghost of a shadow upon it.

Life means all that it ever meant.
It is the same as it ever was.
There is absolute and unbroken continuity.
What is this death but a negligible accident?

Why should I be out of mind because I am out of sight?
I am but waiting for you, for an interval,
somewhere very near,
just round the corner.

All is well.
Nothing is hurt; nothing is lost.
One brief moment and all will be as it was before.
How we shall laugh at the trouble of
parting when we meet again!

About the Authors

Bestselling author PATRICIA SCANLAN was born in Dublin, and still resides there. Her novels, including the renowned *City Girl* trilogy, have sold over 1.4 million copies in Ireland alone, and several million more worldwide, and her work is translated in many languages. Her most recent novels include *With All My Love, A Time For Friends*, and *Orange Blossom Days*, and she is series editor and contributing author to the award-winning Open Door Literacy Series. Patricia has had an abiding interest in Metaphysical and Esoteric studies for many years and her spiritual book, *Winter Blessings*, was another bestseller. Writing *Bringing Death to Life* with her best friends and soul family, fellow authors Aidan Story, Pamela Young and Dr. Mary Helen Hensley, is the culmination of a spiritual journey together, which has been inspiring, invigorating, hilarious, and very rewarding.

www.facebook.com/PatriciaScanlanAuthor
Twitter @patriciascanl18

DR. MARY HELEN HENSLEY is one of Ireland's most sought-after metaphysical healers and synergistic speakers, having emigrated there from the US in 1999. Following a near-death experience in 1991, an ability she'd had since childhood of communicating with those in spirit significantly increased. Overnight, she found herself able to "read" the ethereal field of an individual, linking her to the person's history, gaining insights into how past experiences were creating a person's present reality, regarding their physical, emotional and spiritual health. By creating a new awareness, Mary Helen has helped her clients and readers turn anguish to insight, distress to discernment and heartbreak to healing.

Mary Helen has also assisted numerous people with experiencing the death-process with grace, dignity and understanding, bringing perspective to life lessons, removing the fear that is so often associated with crossing over. Here she shares that wealth of knowledge. The complete story of her life and death experiences can be found in her book, *Promised By Heaven*.

www.facebook.com/DrMaryHelenHensley
Twitter: @docmhh • YouTube: DrMaryHelenHensley
Website: maryhelenhensley.com

AIDAN STOREY is a leading Angel healer and spiritual therapist, both in Ireland and internationally. Growing up in the suburbs of Dublin, the youngest of a family of seven, Aidan recalls being visited by angels since his earliest memories. Unafraid of the beautiful, luminous spirits who watched over him, it wasn't until much later that Aidan realised not everyone could see what he could see—and not everyone shared what was to prove to be an exceptional gift for healing. His book *Angels of Divine Light* describes his extraordinary personal journey, when the presence of angels sustained him through years of great turmoil, bringing light and love into his life and the lives of many others. In *Bringing Death to Life*, he shares his immense experience as a healer, dealing regularly with loss and grief, and tells of the angels' vision for what lies beyond this life. Aidan lives in Kildare, Ireland with his husband Murtagh.

www.facebook.com/angelic.ireland.1 • www.aidanstorey.com

PAMELA YOUNG is the daughter of a spirit medium, from her earliest memory Pamela lived in connection to the spirit world—a "gift" that goes back many generations on the female line of her family. This gift intensified after a near-death experience which occurred at a period of deep crisis in her family life. She experienced what it is to be light and love and returned to the earthly world knowing it was not her time to die, but fearless of death. Later, in her fifties, she experienced a nine-month period where, in meditation, she received messages, via words and visions, from beyond the veil about "The Work of Light and Human Consciousness."

A grandmother of three, the graduate of English and Philosophy is also a retired social worker who now devotes her time to spiritual development, enjoying meditation, walking in nature, silence and sending love out to the planet. From Lancashire, she also volunteers at The Monastery, Manchester, a beautiful temple of Light which awakens the spirit within. Here, Pamela shares knowledge gained from communing with Spirit, including messages from the female deity "Our Lady of Light."

Rainbow Ridge Books publishes spiritual, metaphysical, and self-help titles, and is distributed by Square One Publishers in Garden City Park, New York.

To contact authors and editors, peruse our titles, and see submission guidelines, please visit our website at www.rainbowridgebooks.com.

For orders and catalogs, please call toll-free: (877) 900-BOOK.